NEW POVERTY

Recent Titles in
Contributions in Sociology

NEW POVERTY

———————■———————

Families in Postmodern Society

David Cheal

Contributions in Sociology, Number 115
Dan A. Chekki, Series Adviser

GREENWOOD PRESS
Westport, Connecticut • London

Library of Congress Cataloging-in-Publication Data

Cheal, David J.
    New poverty : families in postmodern society / David Cheal.
       p.   cm. — (Contributions in sociology, ISSN 0084–9278 ; no.
115)
    Includes bibliographical references and index.
    ISBN 0–313–29444–5 (alk. paper)
    1. Poverty. 2. Poor. 3. Family. 4. Poverty—United States.
5. Poverty—Canada. 6. Poor—United States. 7. Poor—Canada.
8. Family—Economic aspects—United States. 9. Family—Economic
aspects—Canada. 10. Postmodernism—Social aspects. 11. United
States—Economic conditions. 12. Canada—Economic conditions.
I. Title. II. Series.
HC79.P6C44   1996
362.5'0973—dc20   95–50520

British Library Cataloguing in Publication Data is available.

Library of Congress Catalog Card Number: 95–50520
ISBN: 0–313–29444–5
ISSN: 0084-9278

First published in 1996

Greenwood Press, 88 Post Road West, Westport, CT 06881
An imprint of Greenwood Publishing Group, Inc.

Printed in the United States of America

The paper used in this book complies with the
Permanent Paper Standard issued by the National
Information Standards Organization (Z39.48–1984).

10 9 8 7 6 5 4 3

For my mother and father,
and the experience they gave me of growing up in a large family

It was not a lack of progress but, on the contrary, development . . . that created the possibility of total war, totalitarianisms, the growing gap between the wealth of the North and the impoverished South, unemployment and the "new poor."

— Jean-François Lyotard, 1993, p. 82

Contents

Illustrations

TABLES

FIGURES

Preface

This book is intended to inspire serious, critical reflection on the relationships between current family situations and the risks of being poor today. There are many reasons for concern. Some of them are: the existence of a life course poverty gradient, in which the risk of poverty is highest in early childhood; the fact that families with children do not appear to benefit significantly from government income redistribution; and the politics of fiscal programs that both alleviate and increase poverty risks, for different groups.

The waning interest of governments in supporting poor people forces us to reexamine some fundamental understandings about modernization and progress. In this book, specific causes of poverty are located within a broader context of problems in modernity. The author argues that the sociology of poverty has entered a new, postmodern phase.

Chapters 1 and 2 contain general discussions about the cultural and political significance of poverty research. The main theme in those chapters can be stated very simply. It is that new forms of poverty can be fully understood only in the context of theories of social change.

Poverty as it exists today evidently has something to do with a special set of changes known collectively as modernization. But what is the connection, exactly? The most common answer is that poverty is due to certain imperfections in the process of modernization itself. Further, it is hoped that correcting those imperfections can reduce the impact of poverty. Three theories of modernization are examined in Chapter 1. They are: standard modernization theory, critical modernization theory, and radical modernization theory. A fourth theory is also considered, namely, that of postmodernization.

In Chapter 2, the history of research on poverty in the twentieth century is briefly reviewed. Poverty research has been closely linked to ideas about progress, in the belief that accurate information is the basis for solving social problems. In the first half of the twentieth century, poverty was seen as a pervasive condition affecting large numbers of working-class people. In the post–World War II period, it came to be seen as a problem of excluded minorities. More recently, views about the poor have been colored by the perception that attempts to solve the problem of poverty have failed. That perception is often linked to fears about the breakdown of the modern family and the emergence of an urban underclass.

Families, and especially families with children, have become focal points for discussions of contemporary poverty in the United States and Canada. Chapter 3 introduces original data on poverty in these two countries that were produced especially for this book. The origins of the data and the methods of analysis are described; the research procedures and the scientific logic behind them are discussed as well. Chapter 3 is written in a straightforward manner, with few technical details. It should be accessible to most readers.

Chapter 4 opens the research issues covered in this book, by describing poverty in female-headed families after the breakdown of relationships through separation or divorce. It is well known that the current incomes of families headed by separated and divorced mothers are relatively low. Attention is also drawn here to their long-term economic insecurity due to low capital formation or, possibly, capital loss. Families headed by women have low levels of home ownership, they save very little, and they make extremely low payments into financial security plans.

In Chapter 5, discussion of children in poverty is extended from just one type of family to include children in all families. The focus here is on the extent to which estimates of the volume of child poverty are affected by particular statistical procedures. The implications of these procedures for child and family income transfer policies are discussed. It is concluded that families with children in Canada and the United States do not benefit substantially from income redistribution and that children from large families are still the most likely to be poor.

From Chapter 6 through Chapter 8 the emphasis shifts from looking at families and children to looking at family work systems and employment income. Chapter 6 examines the relationship between different forms of wage labor and household income. Lack of regular employment and working for only part of the year are the principal causes of low household income today. The interaction between employment activity and marital status is explored. Poverty is found mainly in those households in which individuals not having significant market incomes also do not have strong family financial supports. Such individuals have little informal protection against the risks of the labor market, and they are overrepresented among the poor. Never-married individuals living on their own are especially vulnerable.

Although single persons may have a higher incidence of poverty, there are nevertheless many married couples who are also poor. In Chapter 7, the "shallow income pools" found among the married poor are studied, and they are compared with the large combined incomes in successful dual-career families. It is argued that the latter family type is the result of an intensification of work in the nonelderly population. A result of this process is that less work-intensive families have become marginalized. Such families in 1992 relied heavily on state income-support programs, which have since been reduced.

In contrast to reductions in certain income-support programs for the nonelderly, income transfers to the elderly have remained substantially the same in recent years. The contrasting fortunes of the elderly and the nonelderly is the principal theme in Chapter 8, where information is presented about a life course poverty gradient. Poverty rates are highest among children, and with increasing age more people tend to escape from poverty. Once they have escaped from the poverty of childhood and youth, most people in the United States and Canada are unlikely ever to be at such high risk of impoverishment again.

The role of the state in setting implicit income policies has surfaced in Chapter 8 and earlier in Chapters 5 and 7. It is brought to the fore in Chapter 9, which is the last research chapter. In Chapter 9, evidence is presented to show that in the late twentieth century the state has both alleviated poverty and increased the risk of poverty, for different groups. As a result, intergenerational inequity in social program outcomes is described as an especially troubling issue.

In the final chapter, the author returns to the themes with which the book began. Evidence for and against the three theories of modernization is reviewed, drawing on results from the research chapters. The conclusion drawn is that all three theories have some supporting evidence, or, better put, there is some evidence that can be interpreted so as to support each theory. However, each of the theories also appears to have significant limitations.

The common difficulty in all modernization theories is their failure to give adequate recognition to imbalances and tensions in state income-support systems. The myth of the essentially beneficial role of the welfare state in income redistribution is a central component in the sociology of modernity. It is difficult to see how theories of the modernization of social life can be maintained once that myth is given up.

The hypothesis is, therefore, advanced that "new poverty" is due to a process of postmodernization. In postmodernity, incompatible models of social time generate a series of relational, demographic, economic, and political crises. Poverty groups are formed in those crises. Today, they are formed especially in the crisis of the political economy of the state. More modernization is not going to fix that problem.

Acknowledgments

The research on which this book is based was financially supported by a grant from the Social Sciences and Humanities Research Council of Canada. The Council's long-term support is gratefully acknowledged. Additional support was provided by the University of Winnipeg and Canadian Policy Research Networks.

The data analysis is based on a Statistics Canada microdata tape containing anonymized data collected in the 1992 Family Expenditure Survey, as well as a U.S. Bureau of Labor Statistics microdata tape containing anonymized data collected in the 1992 Consumer Expenditure Survey. All computations on these microdata were prepared by David Cheal. The responsibility for the use and interpretation of these data is entirely that of the author. Data analysis, as well as the preparation of tables and figures, was assisted by Karen Kampen. Her energy and her desire to learn were vital to the completion of many different undertakings.

Some of the early theoretical work for this book benefited from invitations to speak at the Theory Construction and Research Methodology Workshop at the 1992 Annual Conference of the National Council on Family Relations in Orlando and at a conference on family sociology in Oslo in 1994. The latter conference arrangements were made possible by a grant from the Research Council of Norway. I would like to thank Arnlaug Leira for agreeing to the use made in this book of portions of the paper presented on that occasion.

1

Families in Postmodernity

Throwing money at social problems is no longer popular. In particular, giving money to the poor is now often seen as an act of dubious value, for which political consent is only grudgingly given. Of course, the income safety nets in the United States and Canada have always had some large holes in them. Even so, there is something new about our reluctance to support poor people today. Opinions about the deserving poor and the undeserving poor have hardened, and the commitment to maintaining a minimum standard of living for all families has softened.

Current debates about poverty are of interest not only to policy makers and the poor themselves but also to anyone who wishes to understand the temper of our times and how that temper has frayed. Slogans such as "the rise of the radical right," and "hard times breed hard politics," explain part of what is happening. But there is a larger set of factors at work. The present moment is a time of great change and great uncertainty. Social institutions, governments, and nations are in a state of flux. Pressures to restructure economic practices are felt in homes as well as in businesses, and major changes have taken place in family life over the past century. Together with the likelihood of further changes, these events are prompting a broad rethinking of established points of view about families and their place in society.

In this book, we will examine some of the economic and social characteristics of poor families in the United States and Canada today. The primary purpose of this research is not to identify new categories of the poor, nor is it to produce a refined analysis of the causes of poverty. Rather, the main purpose of this book is to learn something about the new requirements for a pragmatic political science of poverty. The reasons why we need a new science of poverty at the present time are discussed in the present chapter, in the following chapter, and in the conclusion to this book.

We must begin by examining how the optimistic views that social scientists used to hold about social policies and the policy-making process have come unravelled. That process of unravelling goes beyond individual doubts about the effectiveness of this or that particular policy. It encompasses a broad range of issues, and it reflects deep-seated changes in fundamental world views.

In the present chapter, we will establish the broad cultural context for the rethinking of ideas about poverty that has occurred at the end of the twentieth century. In the following chapter, we will focus more specifically on the research literature about the extent of poverty and its causes. Chapter 2 will show how the sociology of poverty has tracked broad cultural trends of increasing caution about prospects for positive change as well as growing doubts about political solutions to social problems.

The cultural context for moods of optimism and pessimism about social improvement is the shared belief that people have concerning collective organization for positive change or, in other words, modernization. There have been four principal points of view about the possibility of modernization. They are: standard modernization theory, critical modernization theory, radical modernization theory, and postmodernization theory. Each of these theories takes a definite position regarding the possibility of collective improvement through social action. Standard modernization theory is the most optimistic, and postmodernization theory is the most pessimistic. At the risk of over-simplification, we can say that the recent history of social thought in the Anglo-Saxon countries has been from standard modernization theory to postmodernization theory. In other words, the trend has been from optimism to pessimism about the achievements of social policy.

STANDARD MODERNIZATION THEORY

The central concept for all theories of modernization is *modernity* (Habermas, 1981; Baudrillard, 1987; Boyne & Rattansi, 1990). Modernity is the term used to describe the dominant culture during the period of time leading up to, and perhaps including, the present. It is thought to have begun with a breakthrough, or a series of breakthroughs, from all traditional arrangements that had prevailed throughout earlier human history. In modernity the dominant cultural values ceased to be practices inherited from the past. Traditional values were replaced by criteria for improvement, which came to be referred to collectively as "progress."

The concept of modernity has not been in common use in the sociology of the family, with the principal exception of the work of Peter Berger (1977). It is, however, related to two other terms that are more widely used. They are, first, the concept of modern society and, second, the concept of modernization (Featherstone, 1988). Modern societies are societies in which most of the population believes that it has benefited from, or that it will benefit from, progress. Modern individuals support the progressive institutions that promise to improve their lives. The historical transformation by which progressive institutions gradually took shape and gained control over large areas of human existence is seen as a process of modernization.

Sociologists of the family have often been interested in the differences between traditional societies and modern societies (Cheal, 1991). Those interests were made most explicit in the modernization theories that were developed in the United States after World War II. The most notable of the modernization theorists, Alex Inkeles, spelled out in some detail how "family modernism" was part of what he called the "general modernity syndrome" (Inkeles, 1983; Inkeles & Smith, 1974). In his view, modern attitudes are those ways of thinking and feeling that foster individual improvement and that pose few barriers to individuals' aspirations for a better quality of life.

Much of the discussion of family modernism through the 1970s focused on the changing nature of descent ties. The lesser force and extent of kinship obligations outside modern nuclear families is held to permit greater individual mobility (both social and geographical), and to facilitate the accumulation of resources for investment in nuclear family members. A high level of investment in the human capital of children is a notable characteristic of intergenerational relationships in modern families (Moore, 1966). In modernizing societies, children are cultural symbols that represent the future. Investing in children is believed to be a means of guaranteeing that the future will be better than the present. As a result, modern families have sometimes been described as being child-centered. What is meant by this is that there is a relatively great emotional investment in each individual child, and there is also a strong emphasis upon education and the socialization of autonomous individuals (Oechsle & Zoll, 1992). In order to be able to invest more resources in each of their children, modern parents limit the total number of children they have. The lesser fertility of women in modern societies is in turn made possible by rational attitudes of "family planning," together with a willingness to adopt new contraceptive technologies and a reorientation of values away from natalism and toward material advancement.

Standard modernization theorists have tended to claim that modern attitudes toward family life have an affinity with a particular type of family structure, namely the conjugal or nuclear family (Goode, 1963). The ideology of the conjugal family proclaims the right of the individual to choose his or her own spouse, where to live, and which kinship obligations to accept. This type of family has also been theorized to be especially well suited for life in modern industrial societies. According to Kingsley Davis (1966), vertical social mobility that occurs in modern industrial societies breaks traditional families down into nuclear families.

Modern societies bring about changes of many kinds. Modern families are therefore thought to differ from traditional families insofar as the former respond to societal changes by revising the forms of family life. Ruth Shonle Cavan (1974) contrasted the traditional family with the accommodative and innovative modern families. With respect to the latter, she says that the increased employment of married women is a way of gaining freedom from former restraints in order to fulfill personal potential. Seen from a long-term point of view, such trends are theorized as elements in cycles of change that occur in modern societies. These cycles begin with relative stability in families, which are later affected by external changes. Modern families then proceed to change internally through innovation and accommodation, and eventually return to stability, before changing again in the next cycle.

If this is how families work, then poverty is likely to occur only if families fail to adapt successfully to change, and especially if they take on deviant and pathological forms. Given standard modern assumptions about the functionality of nuclear families, nonnuclear family forms such as sole-parent families are seen as inherently problematic. Ronald Fletcher (1988, p. 103), for example, states that economic insecurity and deprivation are most marked in the case of marriage breakdown in working-class families.

Writing from an unambiguously modernist position, Fletcher (1988) has summarized key points in the standard modern approach to the family. The manner in which he does so exposes in particularly blatant form many

of the assumptions that critical modernization theorists and postmodernization theorists consider to be most questionable. His remarks are therefore worth summarizing.

Fletcher believes that the emergence of the modern family has been an
essential part of the historical process of making a new kind of society,
namely a morally principled, democratic, industrial society. He thinks that
the modern family is clearly a considerable improvement upon family
types of the past. First, he claims that there has been an improvement in
relationships within the family, which are now founded on free personal
choice between partners of equal status who are joined by mutual
affection and sensitivity. Second, he believes that improvements within
the family have been supported by wider improvements in the society at
large. Progressive changes include laws to secure the rights of women and
children, and a greater degree of economic security. Finally, Fletcher
holds that all these benefits are made possible by the fact that the form of
the modern family is adapted to an urban industrial society. The modern
family is the type of family that can most effectively advance the well-
being of its members within a modern society. Fletcher's account of the
modern family is therefore one of its essentially progressive nature. But
how realistic is that point of view?

CRISES IN MODERNITY

Theories of modernization and the modern family have been subjected
to a variety of criticisms over the years. One of the more obvious
criticisms to be made of theories of the modern family, such as that
advanced by Fletcher, is their naïve faith in progress. Any improvement in
the quality of relationships over long periods of time must be difficult, if
not impossible, to evaluate. On the other hand, we do know that there are
unacceptable levels of sexual and physical abuse in contemporary
relationships. There are also many families for whom economic insecurity
is still a serious concern. The failure of modern societies to solve such
problems has been noted, and it is claimed that it is those with the least
power, such as children, whose problems are most likely to be neglected
(Denzin, 1987). The basis for optimism about modernity has therefore
been seriously questioned in recent years.

Second, standard modernization theorists' emphasis on the corre-
spondence between a certain type of society and a certain type of family
structure ignores the fact that contemporary western societies contain
many different living arrangements, both family and nonfamily. The idea

that there exists one type of family system, which is normal for modern society because it is well adapted to modern institutions, is difficult to sustain. Greater freedom of personal choice has had profound effects on the institution of marriage, including such disruptive phenomena (from a standard modern point of view) as a higher incidence of divorce. The increasing variety and flexibility of lifestyles in contemporary societies has led the critical modernization theorists to reject standard modernization theory. Instead, they have explored different ways of thinking about the relationship between the individual and society.

CRITICAL MODERNIZATION THEORY

A number of sociologists have attributed the increased frequency of divorce and other changes to a heightened emphasis upon individual well-being and personal autonomy (Liljeström, 1986). European sociologists often refer to this process as "individualization." The trend of the individualization of behavior is described as an extension of the process of structural differentiation in social systems, produced by the continuous pressure for enhanced functioning in modern social life (Höhn & Lüscher, 1988; Nave-Herz, 1989). European debates currently refer to such concerns as issues in critical modernization theory (Chisholm & Du Bois-Reymond, 1993). Here, concepts of individualization and societal destandardization play an important role in analyses of the nature of contemporary social and economic change.

The individualization model of late modernity has been especially popular in recent German social thought, in a critical theory that supports increased autonomy (Kohli, 1986; Buchmann, 1989). Individualization refers to a trend in which people's lives are becoming more diverse due to their being differentiated from each other as autonomous social units. Greater autonomy has been made possible by the loosening of formal and informal social controls or, in other words, by deinstitutionalization. This is seen as a positive development, insofar as individuals are freed from the restraints and constrictions of organized modernity.

The most notable instance of deinstitutionalization is the tendency for the political class in society to give up its right to rule by decree and to withdraw from detailed interventions in the lives of individuals. The all-pervasive interventionist state of organized modernity, which sought to mold the behavior of its citizens into a limited set of predictable choices, is replaced by the "extended liberal" state (Wagner, 1994). Here, the state adopts the more modest role of entering into strategic partnerships with private interests. As a result, policy decisions are more diffuse and social regulation is looser.

The deinstitutionalization of everyday life encourages and accelerates the process of individualization that has been under way in modern societies for a long time. It does so in part because lifestyle diversification allows individuals to choose between alternative ways of living and working. The destandardization of family life increases the freedoms that are open to individuals and expands their sense of individuality and personal autonomy (Buchmann, 1989). Katja Boh expresses this point as follows: "Whatever the existing patterns are, they are characterised by the acceptance of diversity that has given men and women the possibility to choose inside the boundaries of the system of available options the life pattern that is best adapted to their own needs and aspirations" (1989, p. 296).

Destandardization of social action means that such concepts as the family life cycle explain less and less of what actually happens in family life today. It follows that ideas about being "on time" or "off time" in progressing through a set of life cycle stages are also increasingly irrelevant. Critical modernization theorists have therefore drawn renewed attention to the diversity and complexity of contemporary life course choices. Among the important life course choices that must be taken into account are women's decisions about if — or, more usually, when and how — waged employment is to be combined with family and child-care responsibilities (Jones, Marsden, & Tepperman, 1990).

Increased individual autonomy has two contradictory aspects. On one side, it offers more people the opportunity to take advantage of the productivity of modern technologies. On the other side, it produces greater risks of personal failure and greater isolation for those who fail. Rather than resting on a secure place in a stable social order, individuals are asked to engage themselves actively in shaping their lives and social positions in a constantly moving social context (Wagner, 1994). Some individuals will be more successful than others in the process of life course management. People who make poor choices about careers or relationships or who do not allocate their resources efficiently are likely to fall into the bottom level of society, characterized by material want and chronic financial insecurity (Brose, 1989).

Critical modernization theory has clearly moved a long way toward understanding some significant trends in the technologically advanced societies. However, its generally optimistic view of individual life course management is difficult to sustain in contexts of systemic discrimination and the polarization of life chances. Since one or both of those conditions is found in most Western countries, theories of radical modernization have sometimes been advanced instead, especially concerning the position of women.

RADICAL MODERNIZATION THEORY

The problematic position of women in processes of societal modernization has received special attention from radical modernization theorists influenced by feminism. In recent years, a sustained effort has been made to describe the reasons why women's progress has often not been equal to that of men. Gendered family structures, including the unequal responsibilities of women and men for providing unpaid child care, are often implicated as barriers to continued progress by women. When women have the primary responsibility, or especially the sole responsibility, for child care, they often adapt to the pressure of demands on their time by reducing paid employment. This coping strategy has the notable consequence of significantly reducing women's earnings.

In recent years, increasing attention has been paid to the exclusion of women from the centers of modern society due to the gender division of labor (Glendinning & Millar, 1987; Cheal, 1994). The difficulties that mothers have in gaining access to paid work have been emphasized, especially when they have young children (Leira, 1992). In addition, women's wages are less than men's wages on average. Partly for these reasons, and partly because women usually retain the major responsibility for children when marriage ends, women tend to experience a disproportionate fall in disposable income after divorce (Millar, 1988; Maclean, 1991). Increasing divorce rates from the 1960s on led to considerable alarm about the "feminization of poverty" in the 1980s, especially in the United States (Goldberg & Kremen, 1990). The prevalence of female-headed families increased dramatically during this period and, since other groups such as the aged were being lifted out of poverty at a faster rate, the proportion of the poor who were female rose (Garfinkel & McLanahan, 1988). Women who were sole-support mothers fell further behind other groups, not only in the United States but also in Canada (McQuillan, 1992).

Rising anger among women about the feminization of poverty helped fuel a radical critique of standard modernization theory by feminists. Radical modernization theory is largely a response to issues that were neglected in standard modernization theory and in critical modernization theory. Divisions of class, race, and gender have been of little interest to most modernization theorists, and so alternative models were developed to correct those omissions.

According to standard modernization theory, ascribed categories such as male and female sex are becoming less important in modern societies that are based on individual achievement. The radical modernization theorists, on the other hand, emphasize that the modernization of gender is incomplete. They claim that emancipation from the constraints of traditional cultures has been unequal and that it has benefited the members of some social categories, such as men, more than it has helped others, such as women. Lynda Glennon (1979) has argued that women are marginals in modern society, because of their special location between the public and private spheres that were generated by modern social structure. In certain respects, modernization has stimulated and intensified the segregation of men and women into separate spheres. As van Vucht Tijssen has stated, "Modernization can be understood to have created for women precisely the conditions against which feminists have rebelled" (1990, p. 154).

Feminists and others have expressed concern about poverty among women with increasing urgency since the 1970s. Research on women's poverty has been linked to demands to improve women's economic status, by extending to them the kinds of opportunities that many men have taken for granted. The feminist antipoverty crusade, which continues today, is the most recent of the great twentieth-century movements to eradicate poverty. It aims to do so by extending economic, social, and political rights to include all underprivileged groups. The feminist movement continues to believe in the possibility of progress for all, in fulfillment of the promise of modernity. It may be the last modern social movement.

POSTMODERNIZATION THEORY

In recent years, the glittering prospect of progress has been tarnished, and postmodernists have begun to wonder if modernity itself is exhausted. Postmodernization theory casts doubt upon any narrative of a unilinear path of evolution for all societies following the breakthrough from tradition to modernity. Such narratives lie at the heart of modernization theory, but they also provide the foundations for more specific theories from which laws of social development have been derived. All or almost all laws of this kind now tend to be seen as of doubtful validity (Boudon, 1986; Lasch, 1991). In almost every case one or more counterexamples can be found.

The limitations of unilinear development theories are well known to family scholars. One important criticism has been the argument against undue reliance upon theories linking modernization with the inevitability of the nuclear family. This criticism was first advanced by sociologists and social historians studying modified extended families and kinship networks in modern societies (Hareven, 1982). More recently, Stacey (1990) has suggested that current changes in family gender roles have no clear direction, and she argues that this is symptomatic of postmodern families.

The phrase "the post-modern family" was first used by Edward Shorter in the 1970s (1975, p. 276). He dated the emergence of this type of family from the 1960s, when he believed that a fundamental erosion of the nuclear family began. Shorter identified three main aspects of this change. They are the weakening of the links between the generations, a declining commitment to the idea of marriage as a permanent union, and increased difficulties experienced by women in finding meaning in a life based on domestic activities in the home. Unlike the emergence of the modern family, which Shorter attributed to capitalism, he was unable to identify any "master variable" responsible for recent changes. He attributed the weakening of links between the generations mainly to teenagers turning away from their parents and toward their peers; increased divorce he attributed to difficulties in satisfying an enhanced eroticism, as well as to women's increased individualism and economic independence; and the lack of meaning in the domestic sphere was attributed by Shorter to the contemporary ease and lack of challenge in household chores and to women's liberation.

Liberation and the feminist movement also figure prominently in Judith Stacey's account of postmodern families. She says she uses the term "postmodern family" to mean "the contested, ambivalent, and undecided character of contemporary gender and kinship arrangements" (1990, p. 17). In defense of this claim Stacey points out that the modern family system, which was based on the unity of the conjugal couple, has lost its status as both the statistical and the cultural norm. Stacey finds the underlying cause of the present period of family uncertainty in the "structural fragility" of the modern family. Its fragility is due to the fact that the unity of this type of family depends upon the voluntary commitments of its members. Because they are voluntary, conjugal commitments can be redefined, weakened, broken, or abandoned as the partners' interests change. Stacey suggests that the unreliability of individuals' involvements in family relationships is due largely to the decline in productive and reproductive work in the family, which was the basis for common interests in the past.

Stacey's description of the instability of contemporary families differs from earlier theories of family change in her analysis of the prospects for family reorganization (Cheal, 1993a). What makes the present era post-modern, rather than just a moment of disequilibrium within the cycles of modernity, is that contemporary changes do not seem to be serving as a transmission belt from one cultural definition of normal family life to another. The general direction of change appears to be toward more individual emancipation. Most informed observers of family life today offer only cautious predictions that emphasize continued behavioral variety (Hofley, 1990). At the level of everyday family living, contradictions between collective responsibilities and individual responsibilities appear to have been normalized rather than solved, through all the diverse practical strategies that Stacey shows people have invented as ways of dealing with their private problems.

The "postmodern family revolution," as Stacey (1990) calls our present situation, is a revolution only in the sense that it is continuously revolving. We seem to be stuck in a revolving door without any exit. This state of affairs is exemplified by Stacey's claim that second-wave feminism in the United States has both succeeded and failed (see also Carden, 1984). Feminism has succeeded to the extent that expectations about personal relationships held by most women, and many men, are not what they once were. At the same time, Stacey believes, feminists have not succeeded in changing the dominant economic and political institutions in ways that would accommodate all of those changed expectations.

From the 1960s on, feminism served as a midwife for change by providing alternative meanings for women's lives in employment outside the home. Viewed from a feminist perspective, Stacey believes that the fact that no new type of modern family has yet emerged is because the feminist revolution has stalled. Women possessing greater expectations must now deal with husbands, and with larger social institutions, that have changed in some ways but not in others. An important factor in this resistance to change, Stacey thinks, is economic insecurity as Americans struggle to adapt to an increasingly competitive global economy.

Women have responded to today's situation in various ways, producing a volatile family pluralism in which few clear trends can be discerned. Stacey's postmodern families, then, are in a sense postfeminist. They take for granted a revaluation of women's lives, but they often do so within conventional cultural forms.

Stacey's themes of economic dislocation and the recent attempts at revitalization of traditional family values also appear in Norman Denzin's accounts of postmodern families. Denzin is sensitive to contemporary shifts in socioeconomic polarization, and he presents two different models of the postmodern family — one for the urban underclass (1987) and one for the yuppies (1991).

According to Denzin, the postmodern era consists of a series of moments from World War II to the present that include the worldwide economic recessions of the 1970s and 1980s and the emergence of a new, conservative politics of health and morality centered in sexuality and the family (Denzin, 1991, p. ix). Denzin claims that many U.S. families were disrupted by the massive unemployment that began in the 1970s and by the cutbacks in the social welfare system that followed. The common result of those blows, Denzin argues, has been the increased incidence of mother-led families living on welfare. He believes that children in such families are likely to be neglected and that they turn to other sources of stimulation, such as television. The images conveyed on television are remote from these children's lives, however, since they cater to the purchasing power and the lifestyles of yuppies. The young, upwardly mobile couple is a powerful force in postmodern society, Denzin believes, because of the size of its combined income (Denzin, 1991, p. 121). Large incomes enable these couples to enjoy all the pleasures of consumerism, in lifestyles that emphasize material possessions and aesthetic experiences. The contrast between their lifestyles and the lifestyles of welfare families is an extreme example of the economic and cultural polarization found in postmodernity.

POSTMODERNITY

Denzin's and Stacey's sociologies of the postmodern family display several themes that are characteristic of postmodernist thought and that stand in sharp contrast to modernist accounts such as that of Fletcher. There is the waning of optimism and the sense that progress is not guaranteed, certainly not for everyone; there is the undecidability of a culture that is refracted through many different points of view and that makes it increasingly difficult or impossible to arrive at fixed solutions to problems; there is the accelerated pace of change and the constant newness of forms, which raise expectations that are often disappointed; there is the replacement of productive work by consumption as a central life activity for many people, which alters the meanings not only of human actions but also of social policies; and there is the suspicion that even if modernity has not yet come to an end, then at the very least it has taken an unexpected and peculiar turn.

Postmodernist thought in sociology begins from contemporary experiences of pluralism, disorder, and fragmentation that were not predicted by the modern paradigm of universal reason and its attendant theories of societal rationalization (Denzin, 1986; 1987). As the term "postmodern" implies, many postmodernists are inclined to believe that such contemporary experiences are not simply the effects of a temporary phase of disorganization. Rather, they think that not only is a total reorganization of social life not imminent, but it is nowhere in sight — hence their conviction that we must turn our attention to describing the current pluralistic moment as a unique prospect of postmodernity (Heller, 1990; Baber & Allen, 1992).

The term "postmodernity" implies a periodization of a type of culture that comes after modernity, although that is sometimes disputed. When exactly the rupture between modernity and postmodernity can be said to have occurred is also the subject of disagreement. A number of references to a moment of rupture identify the 1960s as the time when a new cultural order began to take shape (Foster, 1983; Hassan, 1987; Featherstone, 1989).

Seen in one aspect, the process of postmodernization appears as a process of cultural collapse that began in the 1960s. The image of an integrated cultural system founded in core values is replaced by images of decanonization, decentering, dispersal, chaos and indeterminacy (Hassan, 1987; Harvey, 1989; Crook, Pakulski, & Waters, 1992; Rosenau, 1992). Up to a certain point, cultural diversity takes the form of a central culture of (what is assumed to be) normal behavior surrounded by a number of peripheral forms that are socially marginalized. Beyond a certain point, the idea of a normal way of life itself begins to lose plausibility (i.e., it is decentered), and cultural diversity now appears as a general cultural fragmentation. Under such conditions, there are no central beliefs or values that can provide a coherent rationale for collective social practices, and meanings become localized in particular discourses around which communities of interest form.

The loose social structures of contemporary societies are partly a result of, and they have also facilitated, the expanded influence of market exchange and commercialism. Postmodern families are heavy consumers of the many products and services produced by advanced capitalist industries, and they are heavy consumers of the messages that are constantly being generated by the mass media (Baudrillard, 1981; Denzin, 1991). One of the implications of this expanded consumerism for family life is that the voices of children are likely to be heard less clearly against the clamor of adult desires. Within postmodern culture, children appear mainly as objects of conspicuous consumption for affluent parents, and inconspicuous consumption by pedophiles. Otherwise they tend to be ignored.

DISCUSSION

In this introductory chapter, the cultural context for ideas about poverty has been described as an evolving set of ideas about modernity and progress. Standard modernization theory is relatively optimistic about the ability of modern societies to solve social problems through collective action. Critical modernization theory and radical modernization theory also tend to believe in the imminent possibility of progress. However, they both have reservations about the negative effects that can arise from concentrations of power and privilege. Postmodernization theory is the most pessimistic viewpoint. It tends to emphasize the uncertainties and frictions that exist in loosely organized social systems and the lack of clear alternatives to current problems.

At the end of the twentieth century, there is not much optimism about modernity. Fear of poverty has increased, because it seems that there is no longer any guarantee of constant improvement in family incomes (Levy & Michel, 1991; McQuillan, 1992). Troubling questions are being raised about the economic and social pressures on contemporary families and about what will happen to them in the future (Wisensale, 1992). The inability of modern societies to solve chronic social problems, such as children living in poverty, is evidence of the failure of modern institutions to support families. Not surprisingly, such problems are reflected in a loss of certainty in theories of social development.

The functional view of the relationship between families and their environments that is found in standard modern theory is no longer tenable. Families have changed in ways that suggest that the nuclear family is no longer a functional necessity — if, indeed, it ever was. Equally importantly, the relationship between the family and other social institutions has changed. Neither the capitalist market economy nor the socialist welfare state provides guaranteed solutions to current problems (Bauman, 1992). In the consumer societies of late capitalism, wage earning is not tied directly or indirectly to biological reproduction but is diffused in ways that permit a much larger and more diverse field of consumption. However, in the long, slow decline of modern welfare states, programs for families with children have not been immune to financial reductions. Indeed, they are sometimes among the first to be cut.

Today there is an urgent need for new theories capable of describing the often chaotic and fragmentary forms taken by contemporary social existence. Such theories are beginning to emerge from current debates about modernity and postmodernity.

Economic and social restructuring, and their consequences, are topics of widespread concern today. Poverty, which had been on the decline for several decades, seems to have suddenly reappeared in our midst, including the highly visible form of homelessness. In one sense, of course, poverty has always been with us. How much of today's poverty is new? And is there now a poverty of postmodernization that is different from poverty during the era of modernization? We will attempt to shed some light on those questions in later chapters. In the next chapter we shall see how social scientific views about poverty have changed during the twentieth century, in a fashion parallel to the postmodernization of social theory.

2

Poverty and Progress

Conquering poverty, and its attendant social evils, has long been considered a mark of progress in modern societies. One of the most highly
publicized examples of this was the War on Poverty that was launched in
the United States in the 1960s. Success in this "war" came to be seen as an
important criterion of national achievement. The eventual public perception that antipoverty programs had failed, especially in dealing with the
problems of urban blacks, contributed much to growing pessimism about
lack of progress felt by U.S. opinion leaders in the 1980s and 1990s (Staff
of the Chicago Tribune, 1986; Kelso, 1994).[1]

In the present chapter we will take a look at how ideas about poverty
have evolved over the past century. Poverty is a highly politicized issue.
Public thinking about the poor is greatly influenced by political movements and by shifts in the balance of power. At the same time, public
perceptions of poverty have been shaped in the twentieth century by the
research findings reported by social scientists. Contemporary ideas about
poverty are therefore partly produced by the agenda and methods of the
social sciences.

Attempts to link attacks on poverty with national goals of social
progress have a long history in the social sciences. At the end of the
nineteenth century, and in the early twentieth century, progressive reformers realized that acting on the problem of poverty required information
derived from social research. Some of the earliest research on poverty was

conducted in England. Techniques of data collection and analysis were used then that were widely imitated later. The research of Seebohm Rowntree, in particular, was exemplary (Podoluk, 1968). Comparing Rowntree's work with more recent writings on poverty helps to illuminate the changing discourse about the poor over the past century.

The scientific study of poverty is one of the oldest continuous topics for investigation in modern social science. Beginning with the work of Charles Booth (1889) in London, students of inequality have continued to describe the conditions of the poor from the nineteenth century up to the present day. Views on poverty have changed over the years, as economic and social conditions changed and as new perspectives emerged. The most important of these changes is that at the end of the nineteenth century poverty was seen as a naturally occurring problem waiting to be solved. By the end of the twentieth century, it was more often seen as a problem for which attempted solutions had proven to be inadequate, ineffective or counterproductive. In this chapter we will see how that change of perspective came about, and we will consider some of its implications.

Nineteenth-century opinions about poverty were divided over its ultimate causes. From one point of view, poverty could be seen as an unfortunate result of the inevitable workings of the labor market. Alternatively, poverty might be attributed to the failure of poor people to manage their affairs better. Laziness or addiction to heavy drinking and other wasteful expenditures were considered along with unequal access to financial resources to be possible causes of poverty.

Throughout most of the twentieth century, the attention of policy makers was focused mainly on barriers to access to financial resources and notably on limitations in the market provision of family incomes. That emphasis was especially strong after the massive economic and social dislocation of the Great Depression of the 1930s (Patterson, 1981). The personal consequences of the Depression were so obviously *not* due to particular individual or family failings that structural explanations of poverty became most prominent.

Subsequently, policy makers acquired a new confidence in their ability to avoid a second Great Depression, through better macroeconomic management. As a result, the emphasis in social thought has swung away from purely environmental causes of poverty to include functional deficiencies of certain types of families. Today, macrosocial and micro-social explanations of poverty are once again competing for recognition.

There has been a further change in thinking about the causes of poverty. The range of macrosocial causes of poverty has widened to recognize the fact that the state is a major economic actor now. The roles played by the state as economic manager and as provider of income support have come under increasing scrutiny. Questions are sometimes raised about whether or not governments actually contribute to the persistence of poverty, through well-intended but misguided policies. After a century of research intended to help prevent poverty, social investigators and policy makers are still struggling to identify feasible, and politically acceptable, solutions.

THE INVENTION OF POVERTY RESEARCH

The most influential early study of poverty was Seebohm Rowntree's (1902) description of the poor in the northern English city of York. Based on a systematic investigation of 11,560 working-class families in 1899, Rowntree conducted an analysis of the extent of poverty as well as its causes. Rowntree distinguished between what he called "primary poverty," which was due to insufficient income, and "secondary poverty," which was due to inappropriate expenditure. His account of primary poverty had a notable impact on sociological inquiries into inequality, because it directed attention to families' relationships with their economic environments.

Rowntree collected information about the earnings of family members, which he combined to estimate their total family income. He also calculated what income was required by families of different sizes to provide the bare minimum of food, clothing, and shelter needed to maintain their physical health. Families whose total income fell below the minimum standard of necessary expenditure (or the "primary poverty line") were judged to be poor. Rowntree concluded that, according to his subsistence definition of living in poverty, 9.9 percent of the population of York in 1899 was below the poverty line. He also acknowledged that making any financial allowance for the social, mental, and moral activities of his fellow human beings would have significantly increased the number of people found to be poor.

Rowntree's definition of poverty, which used basic (or absolute) needs as the defining criterion of living standards, has been superseded for most purposes by a variety of relative definitions. These definitions take into account the gap between family income and some community standard of consumption. Rowntree's more lasting contribution was to break down the analysis of the immediate causes of poverty into distinct household types. His approach paved the way for modern sociological descriptions of the social distribution of poverty.

Rowntree identified six causes of primary poverty in York in 1899. In descending order of importance, they are: the chief wage-earner was in regular work but at low wages (52.0 percent of persons in primary poverty); the family contained a large number of children (22.2 percent of the poor); the person who used to be the chief wage-earner had died (15.6 percent of the poor); the chief wage-earner was too old, or too ill, to engage in regular employment (5.1 percent of the poor); the chief wage-earner had only irregular employment, which was infrequent or involved short hours (2.8 percent of the poor); and the chief wage-earner was unemployed (2.3 percent of the poor).

Rowntree's work had an enormous influence on the understanding of poverty for more than half a century. In particular, he helped to chart the study of change in social problems by repeating his survey of working-class poverty in two further investigations, carried out in York in 1936 and again in 1950 (Rowntree, 1941; Rowntree & Lavers, 1951). His three studies are of great historical significance, for several reasons. One reason is that they spanned the critical phase of twentieth-century modernization during which the welfare state evolved as a major social institution. In 1899, the idea of the welfare state was still struggling to emerge. By the time of Rowntree's third study in 1950, the modern welfare state had come into existence and it could be treated as an appropriate subject for social inquiry.

Rowntree used overlapping, but not identical, methods in his three studies of poverty in York.[2] In his 1936 investigation, Rowntree once again classified the causes of poverty according to household type. Using a somewhat different methodology than that employed in his first study, he produced a new typology. It showed that there had been both change and continuity in the causes of poverty over the preceding four decades.[3]

The main point of continuity between 1899 and 1936 was that in both time periods the principal cause of poverty was the combination of low wages and heavy family responsibilities. Unlike the earlier study, Rowntree's 1936 methodology did not consider these two factors separately. Instead, he joined them in the composite category of wages from regular employment that were insufficient to meet the needs of a family with at least three dependent children. He concluded that this was the cause of poverty for 32.8 percent of poor people in 1936.

In contrast, the principal change discovered by Rowntree between 1899 and 1936 was the great increase in poverty due to unemployment of the chief wage-earner. From the least important factor in 1899, it jumped to the second most important factor in 1936, accounting for 28.6 percent of the poor.

The third most important factor in 1936 was old age. (Rowntree separated old age from illness in his second study). Being age 65 or older was judged to be the cause of 14.7 percent of poor persons falling below the poverty line, despite the fact that by the mid-1930s almost all of the elderly were receiving a pension from the British government. However, the amount of the pension was inadequate for both the single elderly and the married elderly.

The remaining types of poverty identified by Rowntree in 1936 were, in descending order of importance: inadequate household income due to irregular employment of the household head (9.5 percent of the poor); widows who had lost the essential support of their husbands' incomes (7.8 percent of the poor); family heads who were too ill to work (4.1 percent of the poor); and "miscellaneous" (2.5 percent of the poor). Rowntree introduced the latter category for the first time in his 1936 study. It is interesting because it gives a glimpse of a type of poverty that was to become more important in later decades. All of these "miscellaneous" families were headed by women, mainly because their husbands were no longer living with them.[4]

In his final study of poverty in York conducted in 1950, Rowntree documented a major decline in poverty that had occurred in England over the previous 14 years. Rowntree calculated that, in 1936, 17.7 percent of the population of York fell below his revised poverty line.[5] In 1950, his calculations showed that a mere 1.7 percent of the population could be counted as poor. He attributed this dramatic improvement in living conditions in Britain mainly to the disappearance of unemployment as a cause of poverty and also to welfare legislation that protected vulnerable families, especially those with children.

Lack of employment and inadequate earnings accounted for an amazingly small 1 percent of persons in poverty in York in 1950, according to Rowntree. Illness (21.3 percent), death of the chief wage-earner (6.4 percent) and miscellaneous factors (3.2 percent) were interesting, but unremarkable, causes. By far the main cause of poverty in 1950 was old age, accounting for 68.1 percent of the poor. The enormous relative importance of poverty among the elderly in England at mid-century was not due to a huge increase in their numbers, nor was it due to a serious deterioration in their living standards. Rather, it was due to the fact that as other causes of poverty had receded, the elderly were left exposed as a group that was largely outside the labor market and that was only weakly supported by the state. Rowntree's final investigation showed that the economic exclusion of people who were considered too old to work would be an important subject of debate in the second half of the twentieth century.

TOWARD SOCIAL INCLUSION

Rapid economic growth in North America during World War II, and more generally after the war, had an effect on policy makers' views about poverty that was just as significant as that of the Great Depression. Unlike earlier periods, when poverty was seen as a pervasive condition affecting large numbers of working-class people, poverty in the post–World War II period came to be seen as a problem of minorities.

Expanding economies on both sides of the Atlantic meant increasing prosperity for more and more people in the 1950s and 1960s. Optimistic views about progress for all were common. Observers such as Rowntree thought that poverty as a working-class phenomenon was withering away and that it might eventually disappear. Nevertheless, other voices arguing for a different point of view were soon raised. Rowntree's approach to defining poverty came under attack in his own country (Townsend, 1957; 1974), and an international collage of scholars began to revise accepted ideas about the relationship between economic growth and social progress. A number of influential social scientists in Europe and the United States converged on the idea that policies were needed for excluded groups. One of the most influential of these new observers was Gunnar Myrdal.

Myrdal identified an emerging value in U.S. society, that universal liberties and rights should include a decent standard of living and a measure of economic security. Social welfare policy was becoming integrated with economic policy, and the improvement of health, happiness, and efficiency of the people through better living conditions was seen as an important aspect of progress. However, Myrdal concluded that ideals were running far ahead of accomplishments.

Myrdal claimed that the United States contained groups of people who were held apart spatially, socially, and economically from the majority of Americans, who lived in comfortable circumstances. The most serious example of this was what Myrdal referred to as the "caste line" between whites and blacks (Myrdal, 1944). Discrimination existed as a social barrier to intermarriage and miscegenation, which also had the economic effect of limiting access to income and property. The result was that an abnormally large proportion of blacks was poor. Furthermore, Myrdal noted that in a dynamic economy the tendency for blacks to be the last hired and first fired actually meant that their position in the labor market could deteriorate over time. In a far-sighted observation, he noted, "Progress itself seems to work against the Negroes. When work becomes less heavy, less dirty, or less risky, Negroes are displaced. Old-fashioned, low-paying, inefficient enterprises, continually being driven out of competition, are often the only ones that employ much Negro labor" (Myrdal, 1944, p. 206).

Myrdal's ideas on poverty and progress had a long-term influence that went beyond the analysis of racial stratification. The idea that poverty was especially acute among excluded minorities could be applied to a variety of groups that were generally regarded as having unfavorable characteristics. A negative consensus about a group could be based on racial classification, as in the stereotyping of colored minorities, or it might be based on age differences, as in the stereotyping of old people.

Generalizing further, sociologists came to see poverty as a consequence of uneven, and unequal, modernization in a stratified society. Although economic development and growth are the basic factors in poverty reduction, the immediate issue is: Who benefits at what rate from development or growth? (Miller, 1971). From this perspective, the poor came to be seen as "those who lag behind the rest of society in terms of one dimension, or more, of life" (Miller & Roby, 1968). Stated more simply, in the words of the President's National Advisory Committee on Rural Poverty, the poor are "the people left behind" (National Advisory Commission on Rural Poverty, 1968). People who were left behind included racial minorities, people living in rural communities that lacked modern industries, the physically disabled, and old people who had retired from regular employment (Galbraith, 1958; Harp, 1971; Townsend, 1973; 1979).

One of the most forceful and influential exponents of the social exclusion theory of poverty was Michael Harrington (1964). He argued that a new kind of poverty had emerged in America by the 1960s. The "old poverty" had been a normal condition of life for the majority of people in an economically underdeveloped society. The "new poverty," on the other hand, was a poverty of low aspirations among people who had been left behind in the rush to affluence. Harrington called these people "the rejects." They were "victims of an impersonal process that selected some for progress and discriminated against others" (Harrington, 1964, p. 8). Echoing Myrdal's observation on the displacement of racial minorities by technological change, Harrington dramatically proclaimed that for the poor "progress is misery" (p. 12). Technological revolutions did not benefit them but only excluded them from the new jobs for which they were not trained.

Harrington's exposition of the social exclusion theory of poverty was very eloquent. However, the most precise theoretical statement was made by the English sociologist Peter Townsend (1973). Townsend argued that poor people did not constitute a uniform stratum in society but, rather, consisted of a variety of social minorities. He defined a social minority as "individuals or families who have some characteristic in common which marks them off from 'ordinary' people and which prevents them from having access to, or being accorded, certain rights which are available to others, and who therefore are less likely to receive certain kinds and amounts of resources" (Townsend, 1973, p. xi). Townsend argued that sociologists should study how these social minorities are created by particular relationships to the larger social structure.

Social minorities are people who find themselves frequently or regularly treated as second-class citizens. Discrimination against them may be due to ancient prejudices toward people who are physically or culturally different, or it may occur because of impersonal rules made by employers, government officials, and welfare bureaucrats that exclude those whose achievements are thought to have little value. Examples of the former include discrimination against nonwhites in countries where whites are the overwhelming majority of the population. Townsend gave as examples of the latter the distinctions between the "employed" and the "non-employed" and between "economically active" and "economically inactive" individuals (1979).

Policies adopted by society toward minority groups include attempts to manage their numbers and to manage an orderly transition between majority and minority groups. Townsend emphasized that not all minority groups are treated with contempt. Some may be patronized, as the disabled and the elderly have often been. Nevertheless, the result may be the same in both cases, that is, to create a group of people who are treated differently from the majority and who are given access to fewer resources.

Sociologists have sometimes considered the retired elderly to be a social minority, created in part by government policies that encourage and regulate exit from the labor force (Kohli, Rein, Guillemard, & van

Gunsteren, 1991). In Canada, John Myles (1980) has argued that retirement is no longer a process of gradual withdrawal from productive
activity but is a legally sanctioned exclusion from the labor market. Older
workers often continue to be productive. However, employers and
governments frequently induce them to retire, in order to lower wages
bills and in order to make room for younger workers. The result of this
displacement from the labor market is the creation of a structurally
dependent section of the population.

THE POLITICS OF FAILURE

The social creation of dependence on government income support
programs proved to be a major issue in the 1980s and 1990s. During these
two decades the politics of poverty shifted dramatically to the right.
Policies intended to strengthen rights of inclusion began to be eclipsed by
policies intended to infuse more vigor into individual and family
responsibilities. Despite the war on poverty from the mid-1960s through
the early 1970s, women and children living in female-headed families
stayed poor during the 1980s and 1990s. This obdurate form of poverty
had two contradictory political consequences. On the one hand, it inspired
a feminist politics of poverty and gender, with the goal of achieving
further economic progress for women. On the other hand, it led to a
growing concern about the seemingly inexorable increase in dependence
on public agencies by unmarried women with children. This concern was
part of a larger discontent with swelling welfare rolls (Murray, 1984), as
well as a larger fear about the consequences of the breakdown of the
modern nuclear family (Kelso, 1994).

Perceptions of increasing welfare dependence and family breakdown
have contributed to a new politics of poverty (Mead, 1992). The linked
themes in the new politics are a fear of failure — collective or individual
— and a loathing for people who fail. Compared with the old (modern)
politics of poverty, the postmodern politics of failure is less optimistic
about improvements for all, and it is less inclined to see the state as
offering viable solutions to problems. It is also more inclined to
emphasize the personal failings of the poor themselves and to stress that
they will have to find their own solutions to the problems they face.

Today, there is a common belief in many western countries that things
have gone badly wrong. The prevalence of poor people and the cost of
supporting them is one symptom that things are not right. On that point
there is general agreement. Beyond that fact, however, there are often

differences of opinion about the relative influence of specific causes of poverty.

Structural sociologists and some macroeconomists tend to emphasize the collective failures of economic and social institutions to generate adequate incomes for working people. Influenced by this point of view, Michael Harrington revisited the study of U.S. poverty in the 1980s (Harrington, 1984). He argued that there had been three distinct historical systems of poverty during the nineteenth and twentieth centuries. The first type of poverty was the pauperization of the nineteenth-century industrial working class. The structural origins of working-class poverty were analyzed passionately by Karl Marx (1977 [1867]). Its empirical dimensions were described in detail by Seebohm Rowntree, as outlined above.

The second system of poverty, according to Harrington, consisted of the "pockets" of poor people who failed to benefit from the economic abundance in the years between 1945 and 1970. We have seen how these "pockets" of poverty were theorized by social scientists as the effects of social minorities being left behind in the process of modernization.

Finally, there is the third era of poverty, beginning around 1970 in the United States, that was triggered by economic globalization. Harrington argues that the U.S. poor today are suffering from the direct and indirect effects of the international division of labor. Faced with a rising tide of competition from countries with much lower wage rates, U.S. workers are being displaced from many industries. They are also being replaced by intelligent machines in a new technological revolution. Employers are rushing to find new ways of producing more with fewer people, in order to survive in an increasingly competitive marketplace.

Harrington argues that late twentieth-century poverty is different from either of the forms of poverty that preceded it. What is new about the current wave of restructuring is that it does not strike only the classically vulnerable, namely the unskilled and the immigrants with little education. Occupational restructuring has also undermined the economic security of skilled manual workers in heavy industries, as well as white-collar workers engaged in routine information processing whose tasks are taken over by computers.

In Europe, poverty induced by global market restructuring and the new technologies has been dubbed the "new poverty" (Room, Lawson, & Laczko, 1989; Mingione, 1993). The increasing volume and the changing composition of poverty are now major issues of public discussion. In many countries of the European Community, the number of people receiving social assistance doubled between the beginning of the 1970s and the end of the 1980s. At the same time, the composition of the poor changed in similar ways across the countries of western Europe. There are two main changes: a substantial decline in the proportion of the poor who are elderly and a sharp increase in the proportion who are unemployed. The probability of an elderly person being poor has fallen and, although unemployed people are no more likely to be poor than they were in the recent past, their numbers have risen sharply since the 1970s. There is particular concern about high rates of unemployment among young people, because they are often unable to build up insurance entitlements, which are the preferred basis for social security (Mingione & Morlicchio, 1993). There is also a more general concern about the growing numbers of long-term unemployed (Gaffikin & Morrissey, 1992).

Finally, all the recent changes have had a notable indirect effect on the politics of poverty in some countries. Michael Harrington claims that there has been a decline in the U.S. public's capacity for compassion, which is a by-product of growing personal insecurity. The effects of this shift can be seen in policy decisions in many areas (for Canada, see Battle, 1993; McQuaig, 1993). They are also visible in debates about the last theories of poverty that will be discussed in this chapter. As Mead has bluntly stated: "Dependency at the bottom of society, not economic equality, is the issue of the day" (1992, p. ix).

A Nightmare for the Nineties: The Urban Underclass

Enzo Mingione (1993) has concluded that what is really new about the "new poverty" is not the number of poor people or their recent increase. Clearly, there were hard times in the past, such as the Great Depression, when poverty rates were also very high. Rather, what is really new is the apparent lack of any prospect for fundamental improvement. The new poverty seems to be economically and politically intractable. It is chronic, spatially concentrated, and extreme (Devine & Wright, 1993).

The entrenched nature of poverty today has become a major political issue and a major topic for social research, especially in the United States. Inevitably, it has also become linked to, and confounded with, prominent issues in the U.S. policy discourse concerning race, crime, and urban decay (Staff of the Chicago Tribune, 1986). The belief has grown that the key issue to be addressed in social reform is how to halt the expansion of what is now known as the "urban underclass."

The concept of an impoverished underclass that is not integrated into the mainstream institutions of modern society was first introduced by

Gunnar Myrdal. The term was also used later by Peter Townsend. However, it was not a central concept in their work, and it remained undeveloped and undefined. The term "underclass" was given a new lease on life in the early 1980s, when it entered the public policy discourse as a way of focusing attention on people who are permanently poor. Policy makers at that time were not interested in stable, rural poverty. Instead, the term "underclass" was used to describe poverty in the centers of large cities (Katz, 1993).

Inner-city areas in the United States contain a disproportionate number of blacks, who have been referred to by William Julius Wilson (1987) as a "ghetto underclass." Blacks do have a higher rate of poverty than whites, but nevertheless there are also many poor whites in U.S. cities. In the 1990s, as awareness of the extent of urban poverty increased, the term "urban underclass" was adopted by many social scientists to categorize a broad social problem (Jencks & Peterson, 1991; Devine & Wright, 1993).

As often happens in the social sciences, there has been much confusion about what an "underclass" really is, and how it differs from other classes in society. There is no single, generally accepted definition. A useful summary of the major features of the urban underclass has been provided by the U.S. General Accounting Office (1990, p. 1). Research analysts who discuss the issue are usually referring to a group of people with the following characteristics:

They are permanently without connection to the legitimate labor force.

The women in the group are likely to be persistently poor, to experience pro-longed welfare dependency, and to experience high rates of out-of-wedlock births, often starting in the teen years.

The children in the group are likely to be persistently poor and to have above-average school dropout rates.

Some people in the group exhibit disproportionately high rates of criminal behavior; others experience high rates of criminal victimization.

Individuals and families with these characteristics can be found in all geographic areas, but discussions of the underclass usually refer to people who are concentrated in urban neighborhoods and who are predominately black or Hispanic.

Descriptions of the urban underclass sometimes reflect earlier analyses of social minorities who do not have equal access to resources and who are left behind as the economy changes (Kasarda, 1993). In addition, there are two themes in the current literature that depart significantly from the sociologists' social exclusion theories.

A prominent theme in the politics of failure is a critique of the ineffectiveness of government welfare agencies and the belief that they have actually made the problem of poverty worse. There are conservative, liberal, and radical positions on this issue. The conservative position is that welfare programs encourage dependency and that they are followed by a reduction in work effort (Murray, 1984; Mead, 1992). The principal measure advanced to solve this problem has been work enforcement through "workfare" programs (Mead, 1993).

The liberal position is that the problems of the urban underclass have been exposed by an unbalanced welfare state. During the expansionary phase of the welfare state, high benefits were funneled toward other groups whose needs were not as great. With reference to the United States, Mark Stern has claimed, "Social-welfare programs during and after the War on Poverty were much less likely to benefit the urban jobless than other sectors of the population. Ironically, the urban jobless 'fell behind' during the 1970s not because overly generous welfare payments sapped their will to work or uphold family responsibilities, but because other groups grabbed a larger and larger share of the welfare pie" (1993, p. 230).

Finally, the radical position on the failure of the modern welfare state is that the rules and practices of welfare bureaucracies demean and exploit their clients and rob them of self-respect and autonomy (Funiciello, 1993). The solution proposed here is a universal, guaranteed income. A guaranteed income is not discretionary, and it promises to liberate the poor from interference by case managers.

The other prominent theme in recent discussions of poverty, which is significantly different from social exclusion theory, is the way in which certain forms of family life are held to contribute to a high incidence of poverty. One of the connections drawn between race and poverty in U.S. cities is the prevalence of female-headed sole-parent families among blacks (Murray, 1984; Wilson, 1987). Female-headed families tend to be poorer than average, and the high frequency of these families among blacks therefore contributes to greater poverty in that racial group. This issue is not exactly new. Daniel Moynihan (1965) raised the question of the linkage between black family structure and economic failure in the mid-1960s. He provoked a storm of protest, which drove that issue off the policy agenda for almost two decades. When the issue finally returned, it was because social changes had produced many more white families that resembled the black families of the 1960s (Mare & Winship, 1991).

Families and the Welfare State Crisis

Rapid growth in the number of sole-parent families, together with their high level of welfare dependence, has been a lightning rod for the politics of the family in recent years (Bane, 1992). The main reason for this is that a period of rapid and intense change in western family life from the 1960s on was accompanied by a series of fiscal crises that began in the 1970s. The relationship between families and welfare states came under intense scrutiny as governments juggled their budgets and tried to find new ways of cutting the volume of transfer payments (Sgritta, 1989).

Sole-parent families occupy a critical position in the contemporary political economy of marriage and family. They do so partly for the reasons noted earlier and partly because of changing attitudes toward women's roles. In the past, female heads of families were not usually expected to be employed, since it was considered desirable for women to be unpaid care-givers in the home. At a time when almost all women were expected to withdraw from the labor force after they had children, the dependence of unmarried mothers on the state was not thought to be unusual. However, opinions have changed. As more and more married mothers became a permanent part of the labor force, the economic dependence of many unmarried mothers has increasingly seemed to be an anomaly. As a result, the division of responsibility for financial support between family and state, and between different "family" members, is now a major ideological battleground.

Radical modernization theorists are the only people who still believe that social problems such as poverty in sole-parent families can be solved by introducing new and expanded government programs. Nobody listens to them much anymore, outside the feminist movement. The dominant positions today in the war over sole-parent families are staked out by conservatives and liberals.

The conservative position in the war over poverty in sole-parent families has been to decry the breakdown of "family values" (Kelso, 1994). It follows from this point of view that a new emphasis is needed on "strengthening the family," by restoring the sanctity of marriage. The ultimate goal in this moral discourse about family responsibility is to reverse the upward trend in divorce rates and to reduce the number of sole-parent families. The conservative approach has generated strong feelings in certain groups and has produced powerful movements of social reform. However, its reactionary nature raises the question of whether it is possible to reverse established patterns of everyday life by political will alone. A sociologist is entitled to be skeptical on this point.

The liberal position in the war over sole-parent families does not attempt to restore an earlier consensus on the heterosexual nuclear family. Rather, it takes for granted both the variety of contemporary family forms and the shrinking of welfare state programs. It asks only what should be done to restructure the nexus of public and private responsibilities, in order to maximize the benefits from limited resources. For example, one proposal to solve the problem of poverty in female-headed families is to use the power of the state to enforce maintenance payments by "deadbeat dads."

The phrase "deadbeat dad" epitomizes the politics of failure in the 1990s. It symbolizes in dramatic fashion our obsession with other people's personal failings and the costs that they impose on us. It also expresses our numb resignation that nothing that policy makers have done in the past several decades has worked to alter problem behaviors. It is an icon of despair in the bleak political landscape of postmodernity.

DISCUSSION

In Chapter 2, the history of social theory and research on poverty has been briefly reviewed. Beginning at the end of the nineteenth century, we saw how the scientific measurement of poverty drew attention to the magnitude of the problem, mainly as a consequence of low class position. Later, poverty researchers focused on particular groups that were vulnerable, due to their exclusion from the centers of wealth and power. Today, the focus is still on particular sections of the population at risk. Ironically, however, the major emphasis now is on how more of the poor can be excluded from income support programs, on which they are thought to have become too dependent. Suggested causes of dependency include weak family support systems, which are seen as increasingly problematic. At the end of the twentieth century, the failure of some family members (or ex-family members) to provide adequately for other members of their (previous) families is a significant political issue. It is so significant that new laws are constantly being proposed, and sometimes enacted, that affect how incomes are shared. One day we will have to examine seriously how well income sharing is related to social goals and how far it is affected by changes in social policy. Before we reach that point, however, we need to know more about which families are poor and therefore most in need of public intervention.

A limitation of some current debates about families in poverty, such as the underclass debate, is the tendency to focus mainly on sole-parent families. It is true that these families have a high rate of poverty and that poor sole-parent families are often very poor indeed. Nevertheless, they are not the only poor families, and a broad approach to identifying families in poverty is needed. The reasons why people who live in other types of families are sometimes poor can be instructive.

An increase in the number of female-headed families was not the only significant change in family life from the end of World War II through the 1980s. One relevant change is that a traditional anti-poverty strategy of sending children out to work became less effective during this period (Stern, 1993), either because of the declining value of child labor or because of a greater need for extended education for children. More recently, official poverty statistics show that there was an increase in the poverty rate among young married couples in the United States during the 1980s. This was primarily due to a fall in public benefits following reductions in eligibility criteria and payment levels in means-tested programs administered by a number of states (U.S. General Accounting Office, 1992).

One lesson to be learned from these findings is that a broad analysis of families in poverty is needed. We should not overemphasize those types of families whose poverty is sometimes believed to be the product of individual moral failures. Another lesson is that a historical perspective is often useful. It reminds us that there have been a number of changes in family life, some of which began well before the 1960s, and others that are very recent.

In this book, we will compare poverty in the contemporary United States and Canada with poverty in England at the end of the nineteenth century, as described by Seebohm Rowntree. Although this is not, strictly speaking, a historical analysis (since it compares different countries at different points in time), it may help us to see our own times through a historical lens. Is the face of poverty much different for Americans and Canadians today than it was for men and women in England a hundred years ago, as Michael Harrington's historical periodization suggests? If so, in what ways does it differ?

One of the complications in drawing such comparisons is that social scientists employ different techniques for measuring the amount of poverty today than those adopted by Rowntree. This does not mean that comparisons between his work and ours have no value whatsoever. However, it does mean that we have to be clear about the nature of our research methods. We turn to that topic in the next chapter.

NOTES

1. Michael Harrington (1984) has argued that the War on Poverty did not really fail, because it was never implemented as originally planned. It was under-financed and underorganized, but since it was also over sold expectations were raised that could only be disappointed.

2. The methods that Rowntree introduced in 1899 were repeated in 1936. However, in 1936 he also introduced a revised set of procedures, which were used again in 1950.

3. For the purpose of having a direct comparison with his 1899 study, Rowntree conducted a second analysis of the causes of poverty in 1936 using his original method for calculating the primary poverty line. He drew the following comparisons between the two years in the distribution of poverty types: the chief wage-earner is in regular work but at low wages (52.0 percent of the poor in 1899; 9.2 percent of the poor in 1936); the family contains a large number of children (22.2 percent of the poor in 1899; 8.0 percent of the poor in 1936); the person who used to be the chief wage-earner is dead (15.6 percent of the poor in 1899; 9.0 percent of the poor in 1936); the chief wage-earner is too old, or too ill, to engage in regular work (5.1 percent of the poor in 1899; 23.5 percent of the poor in 1936); the chief wage-earner is employed on an irregular basis (2.8 percent of the poor in 1899; 5.9 percent of the poor in 1936); the chief wage-earner was unemployed (2.3 percent of the poor in 1899; 44.5 percent of the poor in 1936). The fact that unemployment was by far the major cause of primary poverty in 1936 is a reflection of the stringency of Rowntree's original method of measuring poverty and the greater depth of poverty associated with being out of work versus most other causes of low income. Only people suffering from extreme economic deprivation were counted as being poor according to his original standard of primary poverty.

4. In his 1899 study of poverty in York, Rowntree included fourteen cases of women who were either deserted by, or separated from, their husbands within the general category of 403 households affected by the "death of chief wage-earner." Assuming that women who supported themselves as a result of desertion or separation had the same average family size as widows, marriage breakdown must have accounted for approximately 0.5 percent of the poor in York in 1899.

5. Rowntree's revised 1936 poverty line was less severe than the bare minimum subsistence standard set for the primary poverty line in 1899. Replicating his earlier method for comparative purposes, Rowntree concluded

that whereas 9.9 percent of the population of York had lived at a subsistence standard of primary poverty in 1899, only 3.9 percent of the population was living in such poverty in 1936.

3

Sorting Out the Poor

Concern about poverty is not confined within national borders. Rather, it is widespread, reflecting common experiences of economic restructuring and family change. Discussions about the "new poor" are based on accumulated statistics from a number of nations (Room, Lawson, & Laczko, 1989). The importance of systematic comparative investigations for the sociology of poverty cannot be overestimated. Sociological knowledge has too often taken the form of theories that make context-free generalizations about modernity, and now postmodernity, but that in practice are applied to data from only one nation. In the field of social policy research, however, the situation is changing fast as comparisons between nations become increasingly common (Smeeding, O'Higgins, & Rainwater, 1990). This internationalization of social policy research has been made possible by growing communication among social scientists in many countries and by the heavy investments that governments have made in research infrastructure.

The availability of socioeconomic microdata from national surveys that use similar methods has greatly enhanced the ability of social scientists to undertake comparative studies of poverty. In the investigations to be reported here, data will be presented for the United States and Canada. Comparing these two countries is interesting because they are similar, yet subtly different.

Citizens of the United States and Canada have comparable average standards of living and educational levels, and their patterns of marriage and family life have recently evolved in similar ways. Nevertheless, their distributions of household income and consumption are not the same (Card & Freeman, 1993). The rate of unemployment in Canada is usually higher than that in the United States; on the other hand, income polarization due to educational differences has been stronger in the United States. More important, for present purposes, is the fact that government transfer payments to people in need were much higher in Canada throughout the 1980s, and they had a bigger impact in reducing the number of families in poverty (Blank & Hanratty, 1993).

The Canadian transfer system has been substantially more effective than the U.S. system in raising people out of poverty. Sole parents with children were strikingly better off in Canada than they were in the United States in the mid-1980s. They started out with more income before transfers and, in addition, they received income support from the state that led to much lower poverty rates.

In this book we will be comparing Canadian and U.S. poverty statistics for the early 1990s. This period seems likely to appear in retrospect as an interesting time of transition for Canadians (Hunsley, 1992). Whereas the 1980s was a lean period in the United States, when federal and state governments resisted pressures to spend, in Canada income-support programs such as unemployment insurance paid out much more in benefits, partly because of the greater number of people not working or retired (see Table 3.1). Unfortunately, the increased cost of Canada's transfer programs was only partially funded by increased revenues, and much of the cost was added to rapidly growing federal and provincial government debts. By the late 1980s a business-oriented politics of retrenchment had taken hold in Canada. In the 1990s, Canadian politicians have increasingly looked to U.S. models for cutting costs, by reducing eligibility and benefit levels. Linda McQuaig (1993) argues that Canada is drifting away from a European-style welfare system and toward the U.S. pattern of minimal social programs. She characterizes this shift bluntly as "the assault on equality in Canada."

TABLE 3.1
Employment Characteristics of Households in
Canada and Consumer Units in the United States

Employment Characteristics	Canada	United States
Employment Status of Reference Person (Percent)		
Working	66.5	71.3
Nonworking/Retired	33.5	28.7
Unmarried Reference Person's Labor Force Participation (Percent)		
Nonworking	45.0	36.1
Partially Employed	21.6	23.6
Fully Employed	33.4	40.3
Married Couple's Labor Force Participation (Percent)		
Nonworking	17.7	15.8
One Partially Employed	9.0	8.9
Both Partially Employed	9.4	6.0
Breadwinner/Homemaker	15.0	19.3
Provider/Coprovider	27.7	24.9
Dual Career	21.2	25.1
Earning Units (Mean)[a]	1.1	1.1

[a]An earning unit or fraction thereof is defined as: a full-time earner, or a part-time earner divided by two. These are added together for all members to get the total number of earning units in the household or consumer unit.

OBSERVING THE POOR

However much governments in the United States and Canada may have failed to solve the problem of poverty, it cannot be said that they have neglected the need for research on the poor. Rowntree's pioneer work done in England at the end of the nineteenth century was a seminal influence. Rowntree's approach to defining and measuring poverty as a social problem had an enormous influence in the Anglo-Saxon countries. His ideas were quickly introduced into the United States by Robert Hunter (1904) during the Progressive era of reform. Rowntree's main contribution was to define the poverty line as the amount of household income required to meet a minimum level of basic needs. Calculations of poverty lines continue to be widely used in both government and academic research (Gunderson, 1983; Bane, 1986; Blank & Blinder, 1986; Rodgers, 1986; Smith, 1988; Ross, 1989; National Council of Welfare, 1992).

The measurement of poverty lines has raised a number of difficulties, which have been widely debated over the years. Arguments about definitions of poverty lines are often intense, because they are used to identify the number of people who are poor. This is often a very sensitive political issue, particularly if it appears that the number of poor people has been increasing. Widespread debates over poverty measures therefore continue, in the search for a definition of poverty that is comprehensive, fair, and politically acceptable.

One of the most fundamental arguments is over the continued validity of using earned income as the basis for measuring the poverty line. Household income measures of poverty are known to be unreliable indicators of difficulty in meeting the material needs of everyday life (Mayer & Jencks, 1989). Some of the limitations of household income measures of poverty have been known for a considerable time. In particular, Townsend (1970) pointed out that the development of an adequate theory of poverty requires a reconceptualization of available resources. Problems here include practical difficulties of measuring income satisfactorily and three other issues that are of wider significance.

First, financial resources used to meet family members' daily needs do not consist only of current money incomes. They also include savings and other financial assets and credit, which may be converted into current expenditure. Second, the resources on which people draw to sustain life are not limited only to financial opportunities for purchasing goods and services. Household members may also acquire resources "in kind," with which they meet their needs directly, for example, by exchanging goods and services in local systems of reciprocity. They may also provide, or possess, the means for supporting life themselves, as they do when they own their own homes, grow their own vegetables, or cook their own meals. Third, people may also receive benefits such as housing subsidies, medical services, and income transfers by virtue of social rights through their membership in companies, communities, and especially nation-states.

A great deal of attention has been paid to measurement issues that take account of the above factors (Moon, 1977; Oster, Lake, & Oksman, 1978; Paglin, 1980; Haveman, 1987; Axinn & Stern, 1988; Zopf, 1989). One outcome of the debates in this area has been the growing realization that global indicators of poverty, such as income constraint, must be complemented by direct measures of the particular things that particular people lack (Townsend, 1979, 1987; Mack & Lansley, 1985; Veit-Wilson, 1987; Mayer & Jencks, 1989). Lack of suitable housing, such as overcrowding, has long been considered to be among the more serious characteristics of poor families (Britten, Brown, & Altman, 1941; Clark, French, Dechman, & MacCallum, 1991; Power, 1991; Stone, 1993). In such countries as the United States and Canada, where private home ownership has been the norm, the issue of the social distribution of appropriate housing includes the question of housing tenure.

There is a great deal of interest today in the degree of socioeconomic polarization, in part because of questions about access to affordable housing (Doyle, 1991). Bunting has argued that an important change affecting the social structure of contemporary Canadian cities is an "apparent increasing polarization in the socio-economic structure of our society" (p. 308). This is due to inflation and employment trends as well as the increased number of sole-parent (mainly mother-led) households. Miron (1989) has further suggested that contemporary housing afford-ability and housing tenure polarization problems are due to a broad shift in patterns of household formation. Nontraditional families and unattached individuals with low per capita incomes are more likely to establish independent households now than they were in the past. It appears that the sociodemographic composition of low-income households is changing (McQuillan, 1991). They are experiencing increased housing affordability problems, and the number of low-income homeowners is decreasing. Attention will therefore be paid to the question of home ownership in the present study, as one dimension in a broad approach to poverty.

EXPENDITURE SURVEYS

Multidimensional descriptions of poverty require data sets that contain a variety of information measured at both the individual and the family levels. Some of the most useful data sets are those derived from expendi-ture surveys. They collect information not only on consumption but also on income and other financial matters. The data sets employed in the analyses to be reported here are annual accounts derived from public-use files for the Consumer Expenditure Survey in the United States and the Family Expenditure Survey in Canada. The accounting year in both cases was 1992.

The 1992 Family Expenditure Survey of Canada collected information obtained in January through March 1993 on household spending during 1992. Annual data were obtained by asking the respondent for each household to recall the household's demographic characteristics and expenditures for the previous calendar year. Deriving annual accounts from the 1992 Consumer Expenditure Survey of the United States is more difficult. The Interview Survey asks respondents to recall expenditures only during the previous three months. Unfortunately, aggregating the data for all four quarters of the year is complicated by the fact that the Interview Survey sample is divided into three panels, with partial replacement of the sample in each quarter according to a rotating panel design. Annual estimates comparable to those for the Canadian Family Expenditure Survey were therefore produced by annualizing the data for the third-quarter interviews conducted from July through September 1992.

Expenditure surveys in Canada and in the United States collect information about the economic characteristics of single persons and domestic groups whose members share common elements of consumption, especially housing. In the Consumer Expenditure Survey in the United States, the unit of domestic analysis is referred to as the "consumer unit." A consumer unit comprises either all members of a household who are related by blood, marriage, adoption, or other legal arrangements; a person living alone or sharing a household with others or living as a roomer in a private home or lodging house or in a hotel or motel, but who is financially independent[1]; or two or more persons living together who use their incomes to make joint expenditure decisions (U.S. Bureau of Labor Statistics, 1993). The number of consumer units analyzed for the United States in 1992 is 5,164. In the Family Expenditure Survey in Canada, the unit of analysis is the "household," which is a person or a group of persons occupying one dwelling (Statistics Canada, 1994). The number of households analyzed for Canada in 1992 is 9,492.

The units in the two expenditure surveys are conceptually different, but they are empirically very similar. In practice, only 5 percent of U.S. households contain more than one consumer unit. The two surveys therefore describe populations of domestic units with very similar demographic and employment characteristics (see Tables 3.1 and 3.2).

POVERTY MEASUREMENT

Data from expenditure surveys have tended to be used in studies of poverty mainly for the purpose of calculating poverty lines. By convention, the poverty line refers to a minimum level of income below which people are believed to be in serious economic difficulties. The severity of economic difficulties experienced by households is often

TABLE 3.2
Demographic Characteristics of Households in
Canada and Consumer Units in the United States

Demographic Characteristics	Canada	United States
Family Size (Mean)		
Total Number of Persons	2.6	2.5
Number of Adults Aged 18 or Older	1.9	1.8
Number of Children Aged 0–17	0.7	0.7
Relationship Structure (Percent)		
One Person	21.9	28.9
Married Couple Only	24.2	21.8
Married Couple, with Never-married Children[a]	35.7	26.6
Sole-parent Family[b]	8.4	8.7
Other	9.8	14.0
Generational Composition (Percent)		
1 Adult, No Children[c]	21.9	28.8
1 Adult, Children	5.6	6.1
2 Adults, No Children	29.0	27.9
2 Adults, Children	26.3	24.1
>2 Adults, No Children	10.9	6.8
>2 Adults, Children	6.3	6.3

[a]Never-married children may be any age.
[b]Includes one person and his or her never-married children.
[c]Refers only to children less than 18 years of age.

indicated by the proportion of their household income that is spent on necessities, such as food or shelter. Households that spend a large proportion of their incomes on basic living expenses are considered to be poor.

Although the idea of the poverty line appears to be attractively simple, its simplicity is deceptive (Ruggles, 1990). In fact, poverty lines (or poverty thresholds) can be defined in a number of ways (U.S. Bureau of the Census, 1993). For example, the question of precisely which economic resources should be counted as "income" can be answered in more than one way. In addition, income may be measured before or after taxes, which can produce different conclusions about the relative incidence of poverty in particular social groups, especially in different countries.

A more serious objection, for present purposes, is the fact that poverty thresholds are typically calculated using different procedures in the United States and in Canada. Traditionally, the estimation of poverty lines in the United States has relied mainly on calculations based on the proportion of income spent on food, whereas similar calculations in Canada refer to proportional expenditures on the sum of food, shelter, and clothing (Orshansky, 1965; Ross, 1989). While the Canadian measure has the apparent advantage of greater comprehensiveness, neither measure is so obviously superior to the other that it can be taken as the standard for international comparisons. An alternative approach would therefore seem to be desirable for cross-national research.

A larger philosophical problem with conventional definitions of poverty is the obsession with poverty lines as real economic divisions. Poverty lines are used to determine who "the poor" are, in order to count how many of them there are. This procedure assumes that it makes sense to think of the population as consisting of two parts — "the poor" and "the nonpoor" — as if they were really two distinct groups. Since poverty is defined in different ways in different places, for different purposes, it is obvious that "the poor" do not constitute a unitary group. The poor and the nonpoor are not two distinct sections of the population, as descriptions of the working poor demonstrate (Devine & Wright, 1993). The poor consist of a loose collection of people, whose membership varies according to the measure that is used. The apparent simplicity of thinking about the poor as an absolute number of people is therefore undermined by the fact that the number of poor varies according to how poverty is defined.

In research on poverty, the poor are separated out from other people by a dynamic process of the social construction of social indicators. Different indicators may produce different results, leading to different policy conclusions. Although the search for a perfect definition of the poverty line has been very illuminating, it has now outlived its scientific usefulness. Attention should not be focused on "the poor" as a social category, because the evidence that poverty lines correspond with actual social divisions is not clear. Rather, the emphasis should be on "poverty" as a state of being. The definitional struggles over poverty lines show not only that poverty can be conceptualized in different ways but also that it has different dimensions. Somebody can be income-poor and asset-rich, for example, as some of the elderly and some farmers are said to be.

The fact that choices always have to be made about appropriate measures in poverty research needs to be made as explicit as possible. One way to do that is through the use of multiple indicators. In this study, a number of strategies for measuring poverty will therefore be followed, and their results will be compared. Our primary focus in this book will not be on the poor as such, but on poverty as a multidimensional phenomenon. Using multiple measures of poverty enables us to examine some interesting questions. How much consistency is there between different dimensions of poverty? Are there some social groups that have high rates of poverty on one dimension of the household economy but low rates of poverty on another dimension?

The Household Economy

Households are complex economic systems. As a result, being in difficult economic circumstances can take a variety of forms. One way of thinking about the complexity of the household economy is to analyze it as a system, through which resources, such as money, flow.[2] A household first mobilizes resources, then it manages those resources in certain ways, and finally it uses the outcomes from those resources to satisfy the needs and desires of the household's members. Following this model, we can conceive of poverty as having three interrelated aspects: low resource mobilization, constrained householding practices, and low levels of consumption.

Resource Mobilization

Households need many different kinds of resources, but acquiring a regular money income is undoubtedly the most important. In advanced market societies, such as the United States and Canada, the starting point for all accounts of the household economy is the total income of all household members. To this we must add other money receipts, such as inheritances, to produce the household's *total money receipts*. Some households may also acquire other resources of a nonmonetary kind, including gifts that are given to individual members.

In practice, not all of the resources that household members mobilize through their various economic and social roles are available for use by the household. Deductions of one kind or another are often made at source, particularly in the case of earned income. In order to have a realistic picture of actual disposable household income, therefore, it is necessary to take account of income taxes as well as other compulsory payments collected by governments such as state pension contributions (Ruggeri, Howard, & Bluck, 1994). *Total money receipts after all deductions*, or, in other words, net income, is a particularly important measure in cross-national comparisons because of variations in national taxation regimes. Relatively large deductions in the form of taxes and other government levies are made in Canada compared with the United States (see Table 3.3).

TABLE 3.3
Median Income and Expenditure of Households in
Canada and Consumer Units in the United States

Income and Expenditure (local dollars)	Canada		United States	
	Per Capita	Per Reference Equivalent	Per Capita	Per Reference Equivalent
Income				
Income Before Taxes	15,676.60	24,900.91	11,333.33	17,000.00
Income After Taxes	13,109.67	20,427.14	10,528.50	15,730.42
Total Receipts	16,016.00	25,418.82	11,460.00	17,105.39
Total Receipts After Taxes	13,406.67	20,925.00	10,639.67	15,880.00
Total Receipts After All Deductions	12,969.00	20,118.00	10,041.83	14,908.33
Expenditure				
Total Expenses	11,827.75	18,241.43	8,844.00	12,692.00
Food	2,120.00	3,257.14	1,680.00	2,469.57
Dwelling	2,833.57	4,261.97	2,451.00	3,625.71
Clothes	651.00	1,010.83	296.00	451.43
Health	250.00	384.55	376.00	564.71
Necessities[a]	5,884.90	8,893.89	4,722.00	6,994.29
Living[b]	6,219.00	9,395.29	5,490.00	7,962.00

[a]Necessities expenses = sum of expenditures on food, dwelling and clothes.
[b]Living expenses = necessities expenditures plus expenditures on health care.

Householding Practices

Poor households that are lacking in resources can be expected to experience serious constraints on their householding practices. On average, they will be able to spend less on each item of consumption, which means that their purchases are likely to be fewer and of lesser quality. Furthermore, providing the basic necessities for life will take up a comparatively large proportion of their disposable income, leaving only a small discretionary income for purposes such as leisure pursuits, travel, and education. It is for this reason that spending a high proportion of household income on food, owning or renting a dwelling,[3] and clothing is often considered to be a classic indicator of poverty.

Food, shelter, and clothing are usually the first things that most households try to secure for themselves, because they are essential to staying alive (especially in a cold climate). It is sometimes overlooked that prolongation of life also depends on purchasing goods and services that are required to maintain good health. Although annual health care expenditures are quite small in most cases, that is not equally true for all groups. In particular, the elderly spend more on maintaining their health than younger age groups do. This factor should be taken into account in any intergenerational comparisons of poverty rates.

There is a further reason why the neglect of health care costs in much of the poverty literature needs to be reconsidered. The amount and proportion of income spent on health care is greatly affected by the extent of government subsidization for medicines and medical services. There are considerable national variations here, and this is one area in which the contrast between Canada and the United States is striking (see Tables 3.3 and 3.4).[4] Americans spend more on health care than Canadians do, which adds to their cost of living.

TABLE 3.4
Expenditure as a Percentage of Income Before Taxes and
Total Receipts After All Deductions: Households in
Canada and Consumer Units in the United States

	Canada		United States	
Expenditure	Income Before Taxes	Total Receipts After All Deductions	Income Before Taxes	Total Receipts After All Deductions
Food	13.3	16.4	14.6	16.4
Dwelling	17.8	21.9	21.7	24.7
Clothes	4.1	5.0	2.7	3.1
Health	1.5	1.8	3.1	3.6
Necessities	37.1	45.7	40.6	46.2
Living	39.3	48.5	46.6	52.2

Consumption

Whatever the origins of financial constraints on householding practices are, they almost always produce depressed levels of consumption. One of the most visible forms of consumption in which this effect can be observed is housing. Housing tenure, the value of equity in the home (if any), the number of persons per room, and the type of building construction all reflect, and in turn shape, the level of material well-being enjoyed by the household.

It is difficult to compare the standards of living in different countries on the basis of income and expenditure patterns, owing to currency fluctuations. For this reason, all financial values in the present study are reported in the local currency. Nevertheless, realistic comparisons can be made where certain aspects of household consumption are concerned. Comparing housing conditions in the United States and Canada, for example (see Table 3.5), we find that Canadians are more likely than Americans to live in apartments, presumably due in part to the greater concentration of the former in a few large cities. Nevertheless, the populations of these two countries have remarkably similar levels of home ownership and number of persons per room.

TABLE 3.5
Dwelling Characteristics of Households in
Canada and Consumer Units in the United States

Dwelling Characteristics	Canada	United States
Home Ownership (Percent)	62.5	61.7
Type of Dwelling (Percent)		
Single House	55.4	62.0
Multiple-unit House	14.6	19.1
Apartment	27.2	11.0
Other	2.8	7.9
Number of Persons Per Room (Median)	0.4	0.4

Family Size Adjustment

Using the number of persons per room as an indicator of the quality of the housing experience is better than simply looking at the number of rooms in a dwelling. That is because the former measure takes account of family size as a factor in the amount of pressure on available space. (For data on family size in the United States and Canada, see Table 3.2). Similarly, the number of people in a family should be taken into account in assessing the degree of constraint on expenditures from a given amount of income. The simplest way to do this is to divide the total income by the number of members to produce the amount of income per capita. However, this procedure has been criticized for failing to consider the effects of economies of scale in buying everyday necessities (especially the difference between one-person and two-person households), as well as for ignoring the fact that young children need less food and may be less expensive to maintain than adults in other ways.

As an alternative to per capita calculations, a variety of "equivalence scales" have been recommended as means of adjusting for family size (Ruggles, 1990). Equivalence scales are measures that define the extra consumption costs of each additional family member as a fraction of the costs of the person deemed to be the first family member (i.e., the reference person). Unfortunately, the nature of the particular equivalence scale used can have a large effect on poverty estimates. Since there is no sound reason for preferring one equivalence scale over another, the position taken here is cautious. In addition to per capita calculations, we will use the equivalence scale that has sometimes been employed by Statistics Canada, because it represents a moderate compromise within the range of alternative methods. This procedure for calculating the family size adjustment is as follows: Adjusted family size is the sum of weighted persons whereby the first adult is counted as one person and each additional member aged 16 or over as 0.4 of a person, and each child less than 16 years of age as 0.3 of a person — except in a family of one adult and children only, where the first child is counted as 0.4 of a person (Statistics Canada, 1993, p. 182). Since the first adult, or reference person,[5] is counted as one full person, the standardized statistics produced by following this method are identified here as calculated per reference equivalent (see, e.g., Table 3.3).

Table 3.3 shows that the results are substantially different when the amounts of income and expenditure are calculated per capita versus per reference equivalent. In addition to illustrating the practical point that the analysis techniques used can affect the reported results, this fact also has implications for how the poor are to be identified. Where the median income and expenditure levels for related measures are so different, comparisons must rely less on absolute numbers and more on the underlying properties of distributions. This brings us to the question of how patterns of poverty are to be described.

Patterns of Poverty

There are many reasons for wanting to know about poverty, but sociological inquiries into poverty can ultimately be reduced to three kinds of questions. First, we want to know which social groups are most prevalent among the poor. In particular, it is important to know from which sections of the population the majority of the poor are drawn. This is the question of the *social distribution of poverty*. Second, we want to know which groups are most likely to be poor and which groups are least likely to be poor. This is the question of the *incidence, or rate, of poverty*. Third, we want to know who are the poorest of the poor. Among all the people living in poverty, who are the people who are worst off? This is the question of the *depth of poverty*.

In order to answer questions about the social distribution, incidence and depth of poverty, we need to have some way of judging degrees of poverty. We know that being poor means having a low income and spending a high proportion of income on necessities, but how small does an income have to be before it is considered "too low," and how large does a proportional expenditure have to be before it is considered "too high"?

In recent years, two useful approaches to defining poverty cut-offs have become increasingly common. Both of them will be followed in this study. The first of these approaches divides the sample distribution in question into fifths or tenths. For example, the bottom income quintile (i.e., the fifth of the sample with the lowest incomes), or the bottom income decile (i.e., the tenth of the sample with the lowest incomes) is considered to be poor. This approach is particularly useful for cross-national comparisons of the social distribution of poverty. It avoids having to adjust for national differences in standards of living, and it produces stable findings that are not affected by currency exchange rate fluctuations. However, deciles and quintiles also have the serious disadvantage that the poor always appear statistically as a fixed percentage of the population (i.e., 10 percent or 20 percent). Using this measure alone, it would be impossible to say if one country had more poverty than another, or if poverty had increased or decreased over time within a given country.

The second approach to be followed here overcomes the limitations of using quintiles and deciles while retaining the advantage of being able to make easy and comprehensible cross-national comparisons. It defines the poverty cut-off as a certain level of deviation from the median for the sample. For example, an income that is less than 50 percent of the average for a given country may be considered poor for that country. This "economic distance poverty line" of about half of the median standard of living has emerged as a convenient standard among those who make cross-national comparisons (Smeeding, Rainwater, Rein, Hauser, & Schaber, 1990). A positive feature of this method, for sociological purposes, is that the amount of poverty it identifies is a function of the polarization between economic strata. The greater the income polarization, the larger the number of people who will fall below the poverty cut-off.

A deviation of more than 50 percent from the median is recommended as a benchmark for defining low-income cut-offs, for purposes of describing the social distribution of poverty and analyzing poverty rates. However, using the 50 percent cut-off alone can tell us nothing about the depth of poverty. A companion cut-off is needed to study depth of poverty, in order to say something about how far certain people have fallen into poverty. The research reported here therefore uses two cut-offs for the deviation from the median, at 50 percent and 60 percent (see Tables 3.6–3.8).

In the remaining chapters of this book, the methodologies outlined above will be employed to analyze some of the social characteristics of poverty today. While doing so, a number of comparisons will be drawn between poverty in the United States and poverty in Canada. Before launching into the specific analyses, it will be useful to demonstrate how our methodological tools can be used to make cross-national comparisons.

POVERTY IN THE UNITED STATES AND CANADA

Following the procedures outlined above, Canada and the United States can be compared in the percentage of the population falling more than 50 percent below median levels of income and expenditure (Table 3.6), or falling more than 60 percent below median income and expenditure (Table 3.7), and in the percentage of the population spending greater than 50 percent or 60 percent above median proportional expenditures on basic living costs (Table 3.8). Employing a variety of measures of income and expenditure, these comparisons lead to several interesting conclusions.

The most important conclusion is that whatever the measure used and whatever the methodology employed, the United States consistently shows a higher incidence of poverty than Canada. This conclusion is

TABLE 3.6
Percentage of Households in Canada and Consumer
Units in the United States More Than 50 Percent
Below Median Income and Expenditure

Income and Expenditure	Canada		United States	
	Per Capita	Per Reference Equivalent	Per Capita	Per Reference Equivalent
Income				
Income Before Taxes	12.3	15.9	18.4	23.4
Income After Taxes	9.2	10.4	20.4	21.9
Total Receipts	12.0	15.7	21.2	23.6
Total Receipts After Taxes	8.7	10.2	20.5	22.0
Total Receipts After All Deductions	8.4	9.3	20.1	20.9
Expenditure				
Total Expenses	6.2	7.5	15.5	12.8
Food	6.0	7.1	12.2	10.8
Dwelling	14.4	11.3	17.9	16.3
Clothes	21.9	23.1	32.0	32.8
Health	29.5	29.1	35.7	34.7
Necessities	5.3	3.5	12.0	9.9
Living	5.0	3.4	12.6	10.0

TABLE 3.7
Percentage of Households in Canada and Consumer
Units in the United States More Than 60 Percent
Below Median Income and Expenditure

Income and Expenditure	Canada		United States	
	Per Capita	Per Reference Equivalent	Per Capita	Per Reference Equivalent
Income				
Income Before Taxes	6.6	8.5	15.0	16.3
Income After Taxes	4.3	4.6	14.6	14.8
Total Receipts	6.4	8.0	15.1	16.2
Total Receipts After Taxes	4.0	4.4	14.6	14.8
Total Receipts After All Deductions	3.9	3.7	14.7	14.4
Expenditure				
Total Expenses	2.5	2.2	9.0	6.8
Food	2.3	3.5	6.9	5.7
Dwelling	8.2	5.4	11.1	9.7
Clothes	16.3	17.6	28.0	28.7
Health	24.7	24.6	32.7	32.0
Necessities	1.8	1.1	6.2	4.3
Living	1.8	1.0	7.2	4.7

TABLE 3.8
Percentage of Households in Canada and Consumer Units in the United States More Than 50 Percent, or More Than 60 Percent, Above Median Expenditure as a Proportion of Income Before Taxes or of Total Receipts After All Deductions

	Canada		United States	
Expenditure	Income Before Taxes	Total Receipts After All Deductions	Income Before Taxes	Total Receipts After All Deductions
More Than 50 Percent Above Median				
Food	22.4	17.1	29.2	28.8
Dwelling	25.9	22.4	28.3	27.1
Clothes	27.9	27.6	36.7	36.1
Health	35.4	34.7	40.2	39.9
Necessities	20.4	12.4	26.4	24.9
Living	20.0	11.6	25.7	24.2
More Than 60 Percent Above Median				
Food	19.0	13.2	26.5	25.7
Dwelling	22.6	18.9	25.1	24.1
Clothes	24.7	24.3	34.3	34.4
Health	33.1	32.4	38.5	38.1
Necessities	17.0	9.2	23.4	21.6
Living	16.6	8.5	22.8	20.8

reinforced by data on overcrowding (i.e., one or more persons per room). In Canada only 3.9 percent of households were overcrowded in 1992, whereas 8.6 percent of consumer units were overcrowded in the United States.

It is particularly noteworthy that the rate of poverty in the United States is higher than that in Canada for income before taxes, and that the difference is even larger for income after taxes. In Canada, the effect of the income taxation system is to reduce economic inequality significantly and, hence, to reduce the rate of poverty as defined here. In the United States, on the other hand, the income taxation system brings about only a minor reduction in the rate of poverty, if any (see Tables 3.6 and 3.7).

A significantly larger fraction of people in the United States than in Canada spend more than 50 percent or more than 60 percent above the national median expenditures for basic living costs as a proportion of their income (see Table 3.8). Approximately half of this difference is due to greater inequality in the distribution of income before taxes in the United States, and approximately half of it is due to the more progressive effect of income taxes and other government deductions in Canada. We will need to keep these national differences in mind as we evaluate the poverty status of various population subgroups.

DISCUSSION

A number of techniques for measuring poverty have been introduced in this chapter. They are based on technical advances in poverty analysis over the past century, which have grown from the large volume of research conducted in this field in many countries. We have already seen in the cross-national comparison between the United States and Canada how the use of a battery of measures makes it possible to draw conclusions that would be difficult to do using only locally defined poverty lines. The advantages of taking a multidimensional approach to studying poverty will be a persistent theme throughout the book.

Using multiple measures of poverty strengthens the analysis in two ways. On the one hand, obtaining uniform results from different measures strengthens the confidence in our conclusions. As the Economic Council of Canada (1992) remarked, the most important question is not which definition of poverty is correct, but rather whether similar conclusions are reached by using different measures. If data based on different aspects of poverty (e.g., low resource mobilization; cf. resource constraint) or on different methodological assumptions (e.g., per capita family size adjustment; cf. reference person equivalent family size adjustment) all produce the same conclusions, then we may be sure that the findings are very robust. This was the case with our finding that poverty is more prevalent in the United States than in Canada.

On the other hand, if the results from following different procedures lead to different conclusions, then the analysis is deepened in a different way. A new problematic is opened up for inquiry, both as to the nature of the underlying empirical conditions and concerning the researchers' theoretical and methodological assumptions. One illustration of the latter point is worth mentioning in conclusion, since it reminds us how much of the political debate over poverty has revolved around distinctions between narrow versus broad definitions of what it means to be poor.

Data presented in this chapter indicate that absolute expenditures on necessities are less polarized than are proportional expenditures. In the United States and in Canada, the number of families who are unable to meet all their basic needs is much smaller than the number who face severe resource constraint. In Canada, for example, only 3–5 percent of families seem likely to have extreme difficulty in meeting their basic needs, whereas a minimum of 12 percent of them face serious constraints on their householding practices due to spending a large proportion of available money on necessities. Neither of these contrasting images of how many poor people there are is the correct one. They reflect different ideas about what living in poverty really means. With that in mind, we are now ready to begin looking at who some of the North Americans in poverty are.

NOTES

1.   In the U.S. Consumer Expenditure Survey, financial independence is determined by behavior with reference to three major expense categories: housing, food, and other living expenses. To be considered financially independent, at least two of the three major expense categories have to be provided entirely or in part by the respondent.

2.   The description of the household economy given here is a simplified version of a model that has been elaborated elsewhere (Cheal, 1990).

3.   In the calculation of necessities expenditures for this study, dwelling costs were defined as principal accommodation expenses, thus excluding expenditures on hotel rooms while travelling and upkeep of a cottage or other vacation home.

4.   Income and expenditure amounts in Table 3.3 and subsequent tables are reported for Canada and the United States in the local currency. These numbers should not be used to judge the relative wealth of the two countries, as no account has been taken of the exchange value of the currencies. (In 1992 the U.S. dollar was worth more than the Canadian dollar.)

5.   The reference person in the Canadian Family Expenditure Survey is the member of the household who is mainly responsible for its financial maintenance. In the U.S. Consumer Expenditure Survey, the reference person is the first person mentioned when the respondent is asked to identify the person, or one of the persons, who owns or rents the home. It should be noted that these procedures introduce a gender bias into personal data about the reference person. In the 1992 U.S. Consumer Expenditure Survey 63 percent of reference persons were men, and in the 1992 Canadian Family Expenditure Survey 58 percent of reference persons were men.

4

Marriage and Its Aftermath

The risk of poverty among women has often depended heavily on the nature of their relationships with men. When males are by convention the breadwinners for their families, it is only through relationships with men that women can gain access to a regular income. Even in societies where women are heavily involved in paid employment, women's earnings are often so much below those of men that there are significant advantages to be gained from sharing men's wages. That is especially true for women with children. Marriage has therefore traditionally been considered essential for the economic security of mothers and children. Mothers without husbands are financially vulnerable today, as they were a century ago. However, the cause of their vulnerability has changed.

Census data for the U.S. population in 1900 show that 77.2 percent of female-headed sole-parent households were headed by widows (Gordon & McLanahan, 1991). In contrast, U.S. Consumer Expenditure Survey data for 1992 show that only 9.4 percent of consumer units headed by a sole support mother were headed by a widow. The majority, that is, 63.2 percent, of these units was headed by separated or divorced women. In the 1990s it is not death but the breakdown of relationships that disrupts marriages and leaves mothers and children at risk of falling into poverty.

At the end of the nineteenth century, there was much concern about poverty among unmarried females. This concern was prompted by the number of women who were left as widows after the premature deaths of their husbands. In his analysis of poverty in England, Rowntree (1902) listed "death of the chief wage earner" as one of the principal causes of poverty. Of households whose income fell below the poverty line, 28 percent were poor for this reason. Analyzed at the household level, this was the second largest cause of poverty, being exceeded only by the number of families in which the chief wage earner was in regular work but at low wages.

At the end of the twentieth century, widowhood is a relatively unimportant cause of poverty in the United States.[1] Consumer units with a widowed reference person of either sex account for only 7.6 percent of the lowest decile of total money receipts after all deductions, with per capita adjustment for family size (10.6 percent adjusted per reference equivalent). This compares with a slightly higher relative frequency of such units for the Consumer Expenditure Survey sample as a whole, 11.3 percent. In the contemporary United States, the widowed are not poorer than other residents.

This does not mean that marital disruption is no longer an important cause of poverty. On the contrary, the disruption of marriage through death, divorce, or separation is responsible for just over one-third of consumer units in the lowest income decile. The striking fact here is the extent to which marriage breakdown and family division have replaced death of a spouse as a major cause of poverty. Approximately one-fourth of consumer units with very low incomes are in that category as a result of separation or divorce.

Widowed men and women in the United States have very low median incomes. Only the separated have median incomes that are lower. However, comparatively few consumer units headed by a widowed person live in deep poverty as a result of income deficiency. This is so even when one applies the income per reference equivalent adjustment, which is a method that tends to make smaller (and especially one-person) units look poorer than larger units. If net income is adjusted per reference equivalent, the percentage of each marital status category falling in the lowest income decile is as follows: married = 5.7 percent; widowed = 9.2 percent; divorced = 11.5 percent; separated = 22.9 percent; and never married = 19.5 percent. If net income is adjusted per capita, the widowed have the smallest percentage of any marital status category in the lowest income decile. However, when the lowest quintile of income per reference equivalent is used as the poverty line, then the widowed do appear to be somewhat poor, being poorer than both the married and the divorced (but neither the separated nor the never married) according to this criterion.

Seventy percent of widowed reference persons own their own homes. This level of home ownership is below that of the married (77.7 percent) but far above the divorced (48.6 percent), the separated (23.1 percent) or the never married (24.3 percent). The widowed spend a larger proportion of their total money receipts after all deductions on dwelling costs than the married, but only about the same as the divorced, the separated and the never married.

Focusing on the relatively low incomes of widows in the United States can be misleading, since it does not address the most distinctive cause of the genuine financial difficulties that many of them face. The most striking economic characteristic of widowed reference persons is the large median proportion of net income that they spend on health costs — 9.5 percent, versus 3.8 percent for the married and a low of only 0.8 percent for the never married. It is partly due to this age-related expenditure pattern that many widowed heads of consumer units in the United States spend excessive amounts of their disposable incomes on living expenses. The widowed and the separated together spend the largest proportions of their net incomes on living expenses (68.4 percent and 68.9 percent, respectively), followed by the divorced (57.1 percent), the never married (55.4 percent), and lastly by the married (47.3 percent).

Among consumer units headed by women, combined living expenses take up 71.2 percent of total money receipts after all deductions for widows, and 65.6 percent of net money receipts for separated and divorced women. Effective health care reform would go a long way toward easing the financial situation for many widows in the United States, though not for separated or divorced female family heads.

The effects of divorce are felt unequally by men and by women. Men are more likely to remarry than women, especially if the latter have children. In addition, men who do not remarry usually have higher incomes than women who remain unattached. Consumer units having a separated or divorced man as the reference person are much less likely to be poor than consumer units with a separated or divorced woman as the reference person.

The overwhelming majority of poor families that are formed as a result of separation or divorce are headed by women. Consumer Expenditure Survey data for the United States in 1992 show that one-fifth of consumer units in the lowest decile of total receipts after all deductions have a separated or divorced female as the reference person. Most of these units are families with children. Consumer units with children that are headed by a separated or divorced woman account for between 14.7 percent (calculated with family size adjusted per reference equivalent) and 18.9 percent (calculated with family size adjusted per capita) of the lowest net income decile in the United States.

POSTMODERN POVERTY

Poverty in sole-parent, largely female-headed families is a serious problem in most countries (Duskin, 1990; Smeeding, Rainwater, Rein, Hauser, & Schaber, 1990; Hudson & Galaway, 1993). For example, sole-parent families generally face greater housing affordability problems than husband-wife families (Statistics Canada, 1984a; Klodawsky & Spector, 1988; Che-Alford, 1990; Filion & Bunting, 1990; Engeland, 1991). In the United States, sole-parent families, especially mother-led families, not only have less family income but they are also more reliant on Aid to Families with Dependent Children, and they are more likely to live in public housing, than are husband-wife families with children (Zill & Rogers, 1988). The high level of welfare dependency of sole-parent families and the rapid growth in the number of these families has made them a lightning rod for U.S. politics of the family (Bane, 1992; Schram, 1994).

No type of poverty is more characteristic of discussions of postmodern family life than that of the female-headed sole-parent family. Edward Shorter (1975) accurately foresaw that marital breakup and divorce would become increasingly common at the end of the twentieth century. However, he underestimated its negative economic consequences for women and children. He seems to have thought that many women who separate from their husbands do so because their jobs enable them to live independently and that, in any event, many of them will eventually remarry. More recent views have been much less optimistic. According to Norman Denzin (1987), the typical postmodern child probably does not know his or her father well and lives with a young mother who does not work. He thinks that postmodern mothers are heavily dependent upon the social services of the welfare state and that they are likely to live in decaying public housing units where their children grow up severely disadvantaged.

Poverty among sole-parent families has become a focal point for late twentieth-century politics of gender, race, and class. That is not only because these families are increasing in numbers, nor is it simply because of the great depth of poverty in many of these families (there may be other families that are just as poor but whose poverty has been made less visible). Rather, the political salience of female-headed sole-parent families arises from the way in which they challenge modern assumptions about what is normal. They test the flexibility of modern institutions and call into question modern societies' conceptions of themselves.

The prevalence of poverty among sole-parent families appears to challenge modern ideologies in three main ways. First, it challenges assumptions about the necessary connections between reason, individual choice, and socioeconomic progress. Second, it challenges the view of modern societies as child-centered societies. Third, it challenges the idea that modern societies are self-regulating systems that are capable of solving their social problems.

One of the most influential assumptions in modern culture is the idea that the capacity for reason, which is possessed by all competent adults, enables them to make decisions that preserve and enhance their own well-being and the well-being of others who depend on them. According to democratic political theory, it is the capacity of individuals to make rational choices for collective improvement that justifies giving people greater liberty. Furthermore, it provides the principal justification for making heavy investments in their education. The faculty of reasoning needs to be sharpened, and the relationship between the individual and society should be well understood, so that career choices and other life course decisions will be based on realistic assessments. In the specific context of family life, faith in the ability of individuals to make choices that are right for them justifies romantic marriage, rather than arranged marriage, and it has legitimized the liberalization of divorce laws and toleration for alternative lifestyles.

All of these modern assumptions about the connections between reason, individual choices, and progress become problematic when significant numbers of people choose to act in ways that impoverish themselves and/or others. The socially created poverty of many contemporary sole-parent families appears to be a case in point. Unlike the period of World War II and its aftermath, the prevalence of poor, female-headed sole-parent families today is not due to external causes of involuntary separation and a high death rate among men. Rather, the prevalence of poor sole-parent families now is largely the result of marriages that did not work and that one or both of the parties decided to terminate.

The second challenge that sole-parent families pose to modernity is to the image we have of modern societies as child-centered societies. One of the more compelling myths of modernity has been the idea that continued progress depends upon raising the next generation to be healthier and smarter than its parents. In sociology, this point of view reached its apogee in Talcott Parsons's account of the functioning of the nuclear family. According to Parsons (1971), the nuclear family, which is composed of husband, wife, and children, is best adapted to modern society, because it is a functionally specialized unit. The socialization of children has a special place within the modern family system, in which great importance is attached to security, discipline, and love (Parsons, 1951).

Increases in the number of sole-parent families appear to contradict the modern myth of continuous improvement in children's lives. The absence of one parent (usually the father) typically undermines what Parsons referred to as the "logistic" basis of the family, that is, the home, its furnishings, its equipment, and so on. Today, there is great concern about the "logistic" disadvantages of sole-parent families and their implications for children (Rashid, 1990a; Canada Mortgage and Housing Corporation, 1994).

The third reassessment of modernity that is provoked by sole-parent families concerns the prevailing image (in the social sciences, at least) of modern societies as self-steering welfare states. Modern societies are thought to engage in the reflexive solution of social problems, through the enactment of social policies. Evidence to support this point of view seems to be provided by the way in which governments everywhere have responded to the problems of sole-parent families. However, the extent and effectiveness of public agency has been limited in some countries, notably in North America. In an interesting analysis of data from the Luxembourg Income Study, Casper, McLanahan, and Garfinkel (1994) report that women are less likely to be poor under three distinct regimes: where the marriage rate is high (e.g., Italy), women's labor force participation rate is high (e.g., Sweden), or the welfare system provides a high income floor for all citizens (e.g., Netherlands). It may be that what is most distinctive about Canada and the United States as well as the other Anglo-Saxon countries is that they do not have a well-defined family policy, an active labor market policy, or a generous welfare policy. In other words, they are countries in which the social agency of the state is relatively weak in most areas. This raises larger questions about the nature of social programs to assist women and children in need.

In recent years there has been a rising tide of criticism about anti-poverty programs, which are seen as inadequate (by the left) or as counterproductive (by the right). Disaffection with the practice, and the idea, of the welfare state is particularly strong in the United States. Why, it was asked, had poverty worsened, despite all the new social programs of the War on Poverty in the 1970s? The answers to that question were often expressed as concern about the growth of an impoverished and morally dangerous "underclass" (Wilson, 1987; Katz, 1993).

The concept of the underclass crystallized fears about a growing number of people in the United States who depend on social assistance because they are permanently outside the labor market and who therefore rely on public support for long periods of time. The increase in families headed by women, and especially families headed by black females, has been a highly visible example of the trend toward more chronic poverty. Female-headed households in the United States are five times as likely as male-headed households to experience five or more years of poverty, and they are seven times as likely to experience ten or more years of poverty (Bianchi, 1993).

Increasing chronicity of poverty has suggested to some observers that modern welfare systems have failed to solve the problem of poverty, in the sense that they do not enable people to become self-sufficient after a reasonable period of public support. Charles Murray (1984), for instance, argues that income-support programs have eroded incentives for work and a stable family life. It is believed that this has contributed to the explosive growth of female-headed African-American families.

The claims made by Murray and others helped to precipitate a loss of faith in the problem-solving capacity of governments, among both liberals and conservatives. Such lack of confidence in the effectiveness of modern institutions is symptomatic of postmodernity. It helps to pave the way for the withdrawal of the state from expensive social programs, and it justifies replacing universal rights for all citizens with coercive policies targeted at chronically dependent minorities (Evans, 1992). In the 1990s the fate of sole-parent families in North America hangs in the balance. On the one hand it is driven by a desire to force single mothers off the welfare rolls, but on the other hand it is stalled by a fear of further disadvantaging their already disadvantaged children. Postmodern policy makers hold out no hope of solving a problem for which the cure may be worse than the disease.

PARENTS' MARITAL STATUS AND LIFE CHANCES

Mothers and children have a special place in modern mythologies. They are seen as vulnerable persons who are in need of protection from the dangers of urban-industrial society. At the end of the nineteenth century and the beginning of the twentieth century, the great concern was young widows with children and orphans with no financial resources. It was feared that widows would fall into a life of moral degradation (i.e., crime, prostitution), and that the children would be raised in an environment that was both materially and spiritually unwholesome (Zelizer, 1979).

At the end of the twentieth century, the most conspicuous characteristic of widows is that their needs are no longer identified with those of children. In the United States in 1992, the typical (median) widow who was the reference person for her consumer unit was 74 years old. Not surprisingly, few widows are responsible for the care of children today. Widows living with children under age 18 comprise less than 1 percent of all consumer units.

In comparison, separated or divorced women living with children are the reference persons for 5.5 percent of all consumer units in the United States.[2] These families account for 15 percent of consumer units with children.

More children now grow up in female-headed sole-parent families formed as a result of separation or divorce than at any other period in our history (Baker, 1994). Nevertheless, most children still live in a two-parent family. How do children who are supported only by their mothers fare economically, compared with children who grow up in families where both parents are present? The answer to this question is very clear. Regardless of the particular measures of poverty used, children who live in consumer units headed by a separated or divorced woman are more likely to be poor than children in husband-wife families.[3] This description is true for all three of the processes of the household economy: resource mobilization (i.e., income), householding practices (i.e., spending), and consumption (i.e., living conditions).

Income

Female-headed families with children tend to have less income than other families. What needs to be clarified is how serious that situation is and what kind of impact it has on the lives of such mothers and their children. Clarification of these issues is assisted by the technical methods for studying income that were described in Chapter 3, especially by adjusting the amount of income for family size.

Simple comparisons of total family income between families of different types can be seriously misleading if they are used to make inferences about degrees of financial difficulty. For example, comparing the total incomes of single persons living alone against the total incomes of single persons with children would underestimate the degree of financial difficulty of the latter, since the presence of children places a greater demand on resources. Conversely, comparing the total incomes of two-parent families with the total incomes of sole-parent families would tend to overestimate the degree of financial difficulty of the latter. The size of family income is strongly affected by the number of income earners in the family, and the presence or absence of a marriage partner is clearly an important factor here. Two-income families may appear to be much better off because they have larger total incomes, even though their incomes have to be shared between two adults rather than used by only one. For these reasons, then, it is most beneficial to use family incomes calculated on a per capita or per reference equivalent basis when comparing levels of financial difficulty between families of different types.

Whichever way the amount of family income is adjusted, the incomes of consumer units with children that are headed by a separated or divorced woman are drastically lower than the incomes of married couples with children. This is so not only for basic income before taxes but also when other money receipts and income tax payments are also taken into account. Median incomes after all deductions per capita for U.S. families with children in 1992 were $8,262 for married-couple families and $4,022 for families led by a separated or divorced mother. The comparable figures for median total net income per reference equivalent were $16,363 for married-couple families and $7,098 for families led by a separated or divorced mother. In other words, separated and divorced mothers and their children in the United States on average have less than half of the disposable income of married parents and their children.

Using the same income measures, families led by a separated or divorced mother are between two times and three and one-half times as likely as married-couple families to fall in the lowest net income quintile or decile. In over half of the consumer units with a separated or divorced mother as the reference person, income is more than 50 percent below the national median, and in over one-third of them the income is more than 60 percent below the national median.

Spending

We know that families headed by separated or divorced mothers have very low incomes in the United States. How is this lack of money reflected in their expenditure patterns? The answer to that question is very interesting. It leads to the conclusion that these families sustain their current standard of living by reducing their future security.

The low income of families that are led by separated or divorced mothers has a much smaller effect on their standard of living than we might expect. Although their median net incomes per capita or per reference equivalent are less than half those of the married couples with children, the median value of their living costs on food, a dwelling, clothes, and health care is just over three-fourths that of two-parent families. Living expenses per capita are $3,582 for consumer units with a separated or divorced mother as the reference person and $4,115 for consumer units with a married parent as the reference person; living expenses per reference equivalent are $6,082 for consumer units led by a separated or divorced mother, compared with $8,070 for consumer units led by a married parent.

Clearly, separated and divorced mothers make a determined effort to maintain the daily consumption of their families at a level as close as possible to that which is considered normal in their community. One result is that they invest relatively little for future needs. Whereas the majority of husband-wife families with children manage to save some money from their incomes, it appears that many families led by separated or divorced mothers do not. Most separated or divorced mothers in the United States spend *all* of their net income. It would seem to be very unlikely that many of them could ever save the down payment toward purchasing a home.

Living Conditions

In a market economy, a family's living conditions depend primarily on the extent of its financial resources within the housing market. It is the capacity to buy desirable housing that determines a family's relationship with the built environment. The availability of subsidized public housing, or social housing, does not alter this situation for most people in the United States and Canada. In the North American societies, the stock of public housing is not very large and it often takes the form of types of housing that are not preferred.

One of the strongest housing preferences in the Anglo-Saxon countries is for private ownership of the family home (Saunders, 1990). Although there is considerable difference of opinion among housing analysts over the significance of private home ownership (e.g., Barlow & Duncan, 1988), in practice many people value it because it provides greater security of tenure as well as a wider choice of dwellings, including some with more space for larger families (Steele, 1979).

For families with children, amount of space and safe access to play areas outdoors are often important considerations. The number of rooms in a dwelling is often a critical factor in determining its suitability for a family of a given size. Housing suitability can therefore be measured by a simple index of crowding or, in other words, the number of persons per room. As for the type of housing, families with children usually prefer a single house with its own land, if they can afford it. Active children are noisy, and in close quarters this can precipitate conflicts with the landlord or the neighbors. For this and other reasons, rooming houses and apartments are often least preferred (van Vliet, 1983). Families with children may also find that they are discriminated against in the rental market for these types of housing.

Finally, the state of repair of a dwelling and the quality of its amenities can affect not only the enjoyment of a home but also the health of its inhabitants (Britten, Brown, & Altman, 1941). In the absence of knowledge about the structural integrity of a building, its age is often a good indicator of the quality of housing. The construction date for a dwelling can therefore be expected to enter into most families' housing decisions.

The U.S. Consumer Expenditure Survey provides information about all of the above factors of living conditions. It is therefore possible to compare families of different types, to see how well they do in obtaining preferred housing.

Table 4.1 shows that married couples with children have a broad housing advantage over separated or divorced women with children. Two-parent families in the United States are more than twice as likely to own their own homes, they are much more likely to live in a single house, and their dwellings are younger on average than the homes of families headed by separated or divorced mothers.

In the United States in the 1990s, almost two-thirds of female sole parents who were the reference persons for their consumer units were separated or divorced. It is largely because of the extreme poverty of this group and because, after the marriage breakup, most children remain with their mothers (Folbre, 1994) that U.S. children growing up in sole-parent families today are so disadvantaged. In the United States in 1992, only one-fourth of the children of female sole parents had the security of living in a dwelling owned by a member of the consumer unit (see Table 4.2). Children living in two-parent families, on the other hand, were almost three times as likely to have the security of private ownership of the family home.

TABLE 4.1
Dwelling Characteristics of Consumer Units with
Children in the United States, for Married
Couples and Separated or Divorced Females

Dwelling Characteristics	Married Couple	Separated/Divorced Female
Home Ownership (Percent)	72.2	30.7
Type of Dwelling (Percent)		
Single House	77.2	45.0
Multiple-unit House	10.9	29.7
Apartment	6.0	16.1
Other	5.9	(9.2)
Date Dwelling Constructed (Median)	1975	1965
Number of Persons Per Room (Median)	0.7	0.6

( ) Indicates cell is <30 cases.

TABLE 4.2
Percentage of Children Living with Homeowners, by
Family Type, in the United States, 1900 and 1992

Family Type[a]	1900[b]	1992
Married Couple	45.4	72.1
Sole Parent	36.2	28.1
Male	42.8	40.7
Female	33.8	25.8
All Children	45.0	60.7

[a]Family type is determined by the marital status of the householder, or Consumer Unit Reference Person.
[b]Gordon and McLanahan (1991).

The housing market in the United States today is clearly stratified along family lines. Nevertheless, separated and divorced mothers appear to be successful in ensuring that their children are not more crowded than those who grow up in families where both parents are present. All types of families with children are more crowded than the national median. However, in this respect, at least, the children of separated or divorced mothers are not conspicuously more disadvantaged than other children.

Nevertheless, the effort made by separated and divorced mothers to attain the community norms of domestic space for their children comes at a price. That price is a very large proportion of income spent on the family dwelling. Whereas median married couples with children spend 23.7 percent of total receipts after all deductions on dwelling costs, median separated or divorced mothers who are the reference persons for their consumer units spend 34.1 percent of their net incomes on housing.

A shelter cost-to-income ratio higher than 30 percent is conventionally taken as indicating a serious housing affordability problem, especially at the low income end. It is therefore obvious that most families led by separated or divorced mothers face severe budgetary constraints. Meeting the cost of the dwelling is no doubt a contributory factor in the shift of resources into current consumption and away from future security provision among these families.

ECONOMIC INSECURITY

Sole-support mothers maintain the quality of life of their families by cutting back on things that are not for immediate use. Unfortunately, some of these items are the very things that, in the long run, might help them to get out of poverty and stay out. We have already seen that separated and divorced mothers are unlikely to be buying, or to have already bought, their own homes. As we would expect, they also spend much less than the married on dwelling additions and renovations, which help homeowners to maintain and sometimes to increase the value of their property. Separated and divorced mothers are therefore much less likely than married mothers to be accumulating real estate equity on which they can draw in their old age.

Similarly, separated and divorced mothers and their children have much less financial protection than two-parent families against the inevitable drops in income that accompany severe injury or illness, old age, and death. Financial security plans may be provided by government agencies, by employers, or by financial services companies. They take two principal forms — insurance against income loss and guaranteed income substitution. Relevant insurance plans include life insurance and other personal insurance, such as mortgage guarantee insurance, accident insurance, and disability insurance (but not health insurance or the insurance of personal property, such as homes or vehicles). Income substitution plans include social security plans and retirement plans, such as government pensions, private pensions, and individual retirement accounts.

Even though payments into financial security plans are often mandated by governments or employers, separated and divorced mothers pay a smaller proportion of their total income into these plans than do married couples. Furthermore, since the incomes of consumer units headed by a separated or divorced mother are much lower than the incomes of consumer units headed by a married person, the absolute difference in their financial security payments is very large. Whether adjusted per capita or per reference equivalent, the value of payments into financial security plans made by separated or divorced mothers' consumer units is less than one-third that made by married couples' consumer units.

The effects of economic insecurity among separated and divorced women who are raising children today are likely to be felt well into the twenty-first century. Indeed, they will probably receive more attention in future years than they do now. A high rate of divorce is a relatively recent social phenomenon in the United States. It has therefore not yet impacted significantly on the support programs for the elderly. Most separated and divorced women in the United States now are under 50 years of age. The financial position of some of them may change as a result of a new job, or a new marriage, but old age for many of these women must be a bleak prospect.

FROM PRIVATE DEPENDENCE
TO PUBLIC DEPENDENCE

Although the future economic dependency of separated and divorced women when they reach old age has not yet received much attention, the same cannot be said of their current reliance on government income support. In the United States, Aid to Families with Dependent Children is largely a program for sole-parent families, and this fact has generated much comment.

It is interesting to compare the United States with Canada in the nature and extent of public income supports for different types of families. Unfortunately, information is not available from the Canadian Family Expenditure Survey public use file for separated and divorced women as a distinct category. These women are combined with the relatively small number of widows to form a composite category made up of previously married women whose marriages have been disrupted in some way. The families of this group of women can be compared with the families of those married women whose marriages are still intact, in Canada and the United States (see Tables 4.3 and 4.4).

TABLE 4.3

Percentage of Families Receiving Social Assistance: Households with Children in Canada and Consumer Units with Children in the United States, by Marital Status of Adult Female

	Canada		United States	
Families	**Married Females**[a]	**Separated, Divorced, Widowed Females**[b]	**Married Females**[a]	**Separated, Divorced, Widowed Females**[b]
All Families with Children, Percent on Welfare	7.2	42.0	5.6	27.7
Families with Children, Female Not in Labor Force, Percent on Welfare	15.5	80.4	11.4	60.0

[a]Reference person or spouse of reference person.
[b]Reference person only.

In the United States, previously married women with children are five times as likely as currently married women with children to be on welfare. In Canada, they are six times as likely. This high level of dependence on welfare has led to questions in both countries about the willingness of previously married women to work to support their families.

From a statistical point of view, there is nothing unusual about the low labor force participation rate of previously married women with children in the United States. Their level of nonparticipation is practically identical with that of currently married women with children. The simplest sociological explanation for their lack of employment is, therefore, the existence of shared definitions of mothering as a home-centered activity in U.S. culture.

TABLE 4.4
Median Transactions Per Capita with Governments for Households with
Children in Canada and Consumer Units with Children in the United
States, by Marital Status of Adult Female

	Canada		United States	
Government Transaction	Married Females[a]	Separated, Divorced, Widowed Females[b]	Married Females[a]	Separated, Divorced, Widowed Females[b]
Cash Flow ($)				
All Families with Children				
Government Transfers	479.00	2,285.25	0.00	0.00
Net Transactions				
with Government	−2,303.50	1,410.00	−1,045.00	138.00
Families with Children, Female Not in Labor Force				
Government Transfers	618.20	4,542.33	0.00	1,948.67
Net Transactions				
with Government	−1,206.75	4,417.67	−567.33	1,828.00
Transfers as a Proportion of Income[c] (Percent)				
All Families with Children	3.9	25.8	0.0	0.0
Families with Children, Female Not in Labor Force	7.1	89.3	0.0	100.0
Families with Children, Member(s) on Welfare	61.3	83.4	36.1	94.3

[a]Reference person or spouse of reference person.
[b]Reference person only.
[c]Income = income before taxes.

The situation in Canada is a little different. There, previously married women with children are indeed somewhat less likely than currently married women with children to be employed. That is because, while married women continued to increase their labor force participation throughout the 1980s, sole-support mothers did not (Crompton, 1994). The reason for this divergence in employment trends is unclear. Until a satisfactory explanation is given, it seems best to conclude that in the early 1990s there was a norm in the North American societies of approximately 30 percent of mothers being out of the labor force in order to concentrate on raising their children.

The big difference between currently married and previously married mothers does not lie in their labor force participation levels. Rather, it lies in the fact that when they are not employed the latter depend mainly on public income transfers, whereas the former depend mainly on private intrafamily income transfers, presumably from their husbands. The families of currently married women with children who are not employed receive much less in government transfers than the families of previously married women. When income taxes and other payments to governments are taken into account, the net transactions with government agencies by the families of currently married mothers who are not employed are negative (i.e., they pay more than they receive). In contrast, the net transactions with governments by the families of previously married mothers who are not employed are very positive (i.e., they receive much more than they pay).

The most striking characteristic of the household economies of previously married mothers and their families is the extent to which private income transfers are replaced by public income transfers. To put the same point in a different way, the moral economy of marriage is replaced by the political economy of the welfare state.

DISCUSSION

In Chapter 4 we have seen why female-headed sole-parent families are a focal point of concern about poverty at the end of the twentieth century. The incomes of these families tend to be low, and they often depend on public income transfers for financial support. Furthermore, they accumulate little real property or financial capital that could protect them from future economic insecurity. Public policies therefore must have a huge impact on this vulnerable section of the population. Unlike some European and Scandinavian countries, governments in Canada and the United States do not have coherent family policies.[4] Nevertheless, their so-called "residualist" welfare states have created a *de facto* policy of supporting certain types of families more than others. Income transfers are targeted at families most in need. That means, among other things, that female-headed sole-parent families receive more financial support than husband-wife families. This unintentional family policy does not fit well with the family values of most politicians, nor of most voters. The result is a grudging level of support that is punctuated by efforts to "get single moms off the welfare rolls."

The contradictory nature of the contemporary politics of the family is worth mentioning here, not in order to enter into "the war over the family," as it has been aptly called by Brigitte and Peter Berger (1983), but in order to comment on its effects. Family support programs in the United States and Canada are not driven by a desire to perfect modern society. They are used only secondarily to compensate for biological disasters (such as the premature death of a family member), or to balance market imperfections (such as the low wages of family breadwinners), or to reward those who support the state (for example, those who produce its citizens). Rather, supports for Canadian and U.S. families are distributed mainly in such a way as to alleviate the more extreme poverty that is created by exogenous changes in family relationships. These changes are the results of *social* processes. They grow out of the nooks and crannies of everyday life, in ways that are only dimly perceived by the state or by any other agent of modernization.

The ongoing social transformation of postmodern families has upset the assumptions of modernity and has altered what many people expected to see as the path of progress in the twentieth century. Compared with the beginning of the twentieth century, the economic security of children living in families of different types has become polarized. In 1900, American children who grew up in sole-parent families headed by females were more than two-thirds as likely as those growing up in two-parent families to enjoy the security of private home ownership (see Table 4.2). In 1992, however, the children of sole-support mothers are only just over one-third as likely as the children of married couples to live in a dwelling owned by a co-resident adult. Married couples in the United States have improved their level of home ownership during this century, but home ownership among female sole-parent families has actually declined. So much for progress.

NOTES

1.   Information on widowhood is not available for Canada in the present study, because it was not identified as a distinct category of marital status in the public use file for the 1992 Family Expenditure Survey. For the same reason, it was not possible to analyze Canadian households with divorced or separated reference persons as a distinct category. Detailed data on marital status are therefore presented only for the United States.

2.   In 74 percent of cases in which a separated or divorced woman with children is the reference person for a consumer unit, the unit is an independent sole-parent family. The remaining 26 percent of female separated or divorced reference persons with children live in complex social groups, containing at least one other adult in addition to any unmarried adult children of the reference person.

3.   Eighty-six percent of husband-wife families with children are nuclear families, consisting of husband, wife, and never-married children. Thirteen percent of husband-wife families with children live in complex units, which include at least one other adult in addition to the marriage partners. Interestingly, just under 1 percent of husband-wife families with children were recorded as sole-parent families, presumably because one of the spouses was living away from home for an extended period of time in connection with occupational or educational pursuits or in prison. The latter families are technically not intact husband-wife consumer units. However, they have been included here because there is probably some long-term financial support between the spouses.

4.   There is a noteworthy exception to the generalization that Canada does not have an explicit family policy. The Province of Québec has articulated more clearly than most jurisdictions in North America how family life is related to national goals. Québec is the only province in Canada to have both an official Family Council, which is a consultative and promotional body, and a Family Secretariat, whose main purpose is to prepare three-year government action plans (Vastel, 1994). The underlying concern here is a nationalistic emphasis on preserving the French language, and hence the French-speaking people, in a continent dominated by Anglo-Saxon culture. Family policy in Québec therefore has a characteristically natalist emphasis.

5

The Birth of Poverty

The disadvantaged lives of children in female-headed sole-parent families have received a lot of publicity. This has led to an increased interest in the effects of family change on children and to a broad concern with child poverty. In the previous chapter we paid special attention to poverty among the children of separated and divorced women. However, it is important to recognize that these are not the only children who may grow up in poverty. We need to take a look at childhood in general, in order to see why the poverty of postmodern children is such a problematic issue.

One of the promises of modernity was the ideal that being born into a particular family should not determine a child's prospects for living a happy and productive life. It was held that, whereas life chances in traditional societies were based on ascription, in modern societies they should be based on achievement. In order to ensure that this was so, the social distribution of resources for children had to be rationalized in two main ways.

First, it was argued that the state should provide the means of enlightenment for all children, by compulsion if necessary. Institutions of mass education were introduced to provide opportunities for individual children to rise above the limitations of their families of origin. It was also argued that economic and cultural resources would have to be redistributed. This was to be done in order that no family could fall so far below the majority that its children would be unable to participate fully in modern institutions. In North America, the second argument was less successful than the first. Where, then, do we stand today?

An international research program on childhood, launched by the European Centre for Social Welfare Policy and Research, has asked about distributive justice between the generations (Qvortrup, 1991). Are resources evenly distributed between the generations, and do children get their fair share? The European program of research on childhood was extended to include Canada, where the issue of distributive justice was evaluated by Robert Glossop (1991). He observed that since 1980 the rate of poverty among children has exceeded the rate of poverty for the population of Canada as a whole, especially children in female-headed sole-parent families. Similar findings have been reported for the United States. The percentage of children in families with an income less than half the U.S. median income for all families rose steadily during the 1970s and 1980s (Bianchi, 1993). One of the most significant changes affecting the economic well-being of children was the increase in sole-parent families. Another significant change is that public assistance programs that benefit families with children now remove fewer children from poverty in the United States than they did two decades ago (Danziger & Weinberg, cited in Bianchi, 1993). It seems that the needs of children have not had high priority in North America in recent years.

DISTRIBUTIVE JUSTICE

Children living in poverty recently have been rediscovered by social researchers and by social policy makers and politicians (Johnson, Sum, & Weill, 1988; Greene, 1991; Marsden, 1991). There is a growing belief that children are relatively disadvantaged members of contemporary societies, yet questions about distributive justice for children (between families with children and families without children, and among families with different numbers of children) are notoriously hard to resolve.

Two principal criteria can be advanced as reasons for believing that one group is not treated fairly in comparison with another. First, it may be considered fair that the rewards of both groups should be proportional to their efforts. People who work harder and who contribute more to society should get more in return. Second, it may be considered fair that the amount of economic support should be proportional to the extent of individuals' needs. Those people with the largest unmet needs require a greater share of available supports in order to have the same quality of life as everyone else.

The first (effort bargain) criterion of distributive justice is rarely applied to children. However, Qvortrup (1991) has argued strongly for recognition of the work that children perform, especially in school where they prepare themselves for adult life. Nevertheless, most observers see children as nonproductive dependents, whose relationship to society is defined mainly by the extent of their needs.

Statistical comparisons of economic well-being between families of different sizes rely heavily upon estimates of relative need. These estimates are usually incorporated into data analysis procedures in the form of adjustments for family size (see Chapter 3). In the simplest procedure, each member of a family is considered to have equal needs, and the distribution of resources is calculated per capita. Alternatively, children are considered to have lesser needs than adults, and "equivalence scales" are constructed that assign weights to children that are a fraction of the weight assigned to an adult. Here, the distribution of resources is typically calculated based on a per reference person equivalent. There are many versions of these equivalence scales in use today. The problem is that estimates of inequality, poverty, and distributive justice can be very sensitive to the nature of the equivalence scale that is used. This point is worth emphasizing, because it has an important implication.

It may seem that the technical choice of a family size adjustment technique is an arcane issue that can be of interest only to statisticians and economists. However, equivalence scales are used not only for academic research alone but also by policy makers who decide how incomes will be redistributed. As Phipps and Garner have noted (1994, p. 14), equivalence scales are being used for almost all tax and transfer policies now. In the contemporary welfare states, equivalence scales that are used in designing government programs enter directly into the official reinforcement of poverty, by helping to define who will be saved from poverty and who will not.

The apparent objectivity of equivalence scales obscures the fact that the assumptions about needs that are implicit in them are social constructs. Children are constructed as lesser beings who have lesser needs than adults. At first glance, the lower weighting given to the needs of children appears to have an obvious validity, which is grounded in the biology of human development. Young children eat less food than adults. They also need less physical space, since babies spend a lot of time sleeping and they are not very mobile until they learn to walk. Beyond these elementary points, however, statistical estimates of the lesser needs of children are usually derived from observations on existing expenditure patterns. These patterns are the results of purchasing decisions that *adults* make, about how much to spend on themselves and how much to spend on children. The relative consumption levels of children and adults are products of the social relationships between them, especially between children and parents. It is the parents who usually decide what their children's diet is, what clothes they wear, and how much domestic space and equipment there is for children's play.

Social science descriptions of the "needs" of children reflect adults' cultural definitions of childhood, which may vary between social groups and from one society to another. More importantly, they reflect the power relationship that gives adults the ability to define the needs of children, but not the reverse.

An instructive example of the empirical variability of children's "needs" concerns the purchase of children's clothing in the United States and Canada. It has sometimes been hypothesized that large families need to spend less money per child on clothing than small families, because the clothes of the oldest daughter and the oldest son can be passed down to their younger siblings. This would appear to be a classic example of the economists' concept of economies of scale in householding. However, in research conducted as part of the present study it was found that the family size hypothesis of falling clothes purchase needs was confirmed only for the United States, not for Canada.

In the United States, the median expenditure on children's clothing per child in families with three or more children was half that of families with only one child. In Canada, however, no such relationship was found. There, families with three or more children spend almost as much on children's clothing per child as do families having only two children or with just a single child. It appears that Canadian parents and American parents do not define their children's clothing needs in the same way.

Evidence that children's needs are socially constructed does not mean that equivalence scales should never be used in family studies. It does mean that they should be used with caution and that their use becomes especially problematic in cross-cultural comparisons. It also makes the simplicity of the adjustment for per capita family size very attractive. It is at least possible to state the theoretical rationale for using the latter procedure precisely. Comparisons of resources per capita enable us to describe for any country the extent to which children are treated unequally by comparison with adults and by comparison with children in other families.

KIDS OR NO KIDS

During the 1980s, it became socially acceptable for married couples to choose not to have children. As a result, attention came to be focused on a new form of social and economic privilege, the double-income-no-kids family better known as "DINKs." It is debatable whether deliberately childless couples were ever numerous enough to contribute much to socioeconomic polarization. However, they certainly helped to increase the sense of relative deprivation among parents who had less discretionary income. The issue of two-income versus one-income families will be examined later in this book. Here we will simply conduct a general comparison of all families who have minor children (i.e., children under age 18) living at home with all families who have no co-resident minor children.

In the United States, families with children are less well off than families without children, whether adjusted income is calculated per capita or per reference equivalent. Median net income per reference equivalent in U.S. consumer units with children is 15 percent below that of consumer units with no children. The shortfall in net income per capita is much larger, at 44 percent. In Canada the differences are smaller, but in the same direction. Median net income per reference equivalent among Canadian households with children is 6 percent less than in households without children, and net income per capita in households with children is a full one-third (33.4 percent) below that in households containing no children.

Differences in average incomes between families with children and families without children are reflected in comparative statistics on the incidence of poverty. In both countries, families with children are more likely than families without children to fall into the lowest decile of total receipts after all deductions (i.e., net income). This pattern is especially strong when net income is adjusted per capita. When income is adjusted per reference equivalent, the pattern of more poverty among families with children is more evident in the United States.

Interestingly, per capita poverty rates for families with and without children are very similar for the United States and Canada. In the United States, 19.0 percent of consumer units with children fall in the lowest decile of net income per capita, whereas only 4.8 percent of consumer units without children do so. In Canada, 19.6 percent of households with children lie in the bottom decile of net income per capita, compared with 4.1 percent of households with no children.

Neutrality toward Natality

The similarity in quantile poverty rates for Canada and the United States appears to be puzzling when it is recalled from Chapter 3 that the Canadian income taxation system has a greater effect in reducing economic inequality than the U.S. taxation system. The apparent paradox is due to the fact that, although the Canadian government has been more effective at reducing the depth of poverty than the U.S. government, it has not done anything more to alter the inequitable distribution of income between families of different types. This point needs careful description.

In the United States, government levies do not have a noteworthy effect on the distribution of family incomes, though they do reduce inequality slightly. In Canada, on the other hand, the effect of taxes and other government deductions has been to reduce the after-tax incomes of the majority of the population in such a way that the net incomes of the poorest families end up closer to the national median. In Canada, approximately one in five households with children (21.1 percent) have per capita income before taxes that is less than half the national median, but, when all government levies are taken into account, only one in six Canadian households with children (16.7 percent) have a per capita income less than 50 percent of the national median.

Although the tax regime in Canada reduces the distance between the poorest families with children and the national median income, it does not remove any of them from the lowest income decile. That is because the Canadian tax system alleviates the fiscal burden on low-income families with and without children in much the same way. In fact, the Canadian tax regime has a more favorable effect on families without children than it does on families with children, whichever way income per person is calculated.

Before taxes, households with no children in Canada are slightly more likely than households with children to have incomes per reference equivalent less than 50 percent of the median Canadian household income (16.4 percent versus 15.1 percent). However, after income taxes and other government levies have been deducted, households with no children are slightly *less* likely than families with children to have less than 50 percent of the national median income (8.8 percent versus 10.1 percent). A similar shift is observable when incomes are calculated per capita. Before taxes, households with no children are only one-third as likely as households with children to have incomes per capita that are less than half the Canadian median (6.9 percent versus 21.1 percent). After taxes, households with no children are a minuscule one-fifth as likely as households with children to have per capita incomes less than half the national median (3.3 percent versus 16.7 percent).

The social effect of government taxation policies in Canada is to reinforce and to strengthen pre-existing income inequalities between families with children and families with no children. The percentage of households with children in the bottom decile of income per reference equivalent is 10.3 percent before taxes and 10.7 percent after taxes; for the bottom decile of income per capita, the comparable figures are 18.0 percent before taxes and 19.6 percent after taxes. In contrast, households with no children see their risk of falling into the bottom decile of income slip marginally from 9.8 percent before taxes to 9.6 percent after taxes per reference equivalent, and from 5.1 percent before taxes to 4.1 percent after taxes per capita.

In the United States, pre-existing income inequalities between families with children and families with no children are not strengthened by the effects of taxes and other government deductions, nor are they reduced. Income inequalities between these families are not altered in any way by taxation policies in the United States, regardless of whether they are calculated per reference equivalent or per capita.

Overall, the stance of the North American tax regimes toward natality is either one of neutrality (the U.S. case) or one of neutrality mixed with mild antinatality (the Canadian case).

Poor Families with Children

It is not immediately obvious why the U.S. and Canadian governments have been so disinterested in the issue of distributive justice between families with children and families without children. They have, after all, repeatedly emphasized their commitment to family values and their support for family care-giving. Nevertheless, the effects of the neglect of families with children are clearly visible in the social distribution of poverty in the United States and in Canada. Families with children are overrepresented among the poor in both countries.

In the United States, families with children comprised a little over one-third (36.6 percent) of all consumer units sampled in the 1992 Consumer Expenditure Survey, yet they made up close to one-half (49.6 percent) of consumer units with net incomes in the lowest decile, with family size adjusted per reference equivalent. When net income was adjusted per capita, nearly seven out of ten (69.4 percent) consumer units in the low-est net income decile consisted of families with children.[1]

In Canada, the prevalence of families with children among the income poor is dramatic when income is calculated per capita. Canadian families with children comprised 38.1 percent of all households studied in the 1992 Family Expenditure Survey. These families were slightly overrepresented in the lowest net income decile when family size was adjusted per reference equivalent, at 40.7 percent. When net income was calculated per capita, families with children made up a huge three-fourths (74.6 percent) of households in the poorest tenth of the sample.

RETHINKING FAMILY SHARING

How far families with children are seen as living in poverty clearly depends on the technical procedures that are used to take account of variable family size. The dominant approach taken by poverty researchers has been to give a lower weighting to the members of large families, on the assumption that they benefit from "economies of scale." The validity of this procedure is questionable.

The notion of efficiencies of scale was derived from early analyses of industrial production. If manufacturing is organized on a large scale, then businesses may be able to lower their costs of production through such stratagems as bulk purchasing of raw materials. This logic provided the rationale for Fordist production methods, whose self-evident efficiencies have been much admired in modern societies. Because of their prestige, Fordist assumptions have sometimes been reflected uncritically in accounts of systems of social provisioning that have very different sociological properties.

Modern neoclassical economics is concerned above all with maximizing the relationship between the value of system inputs and the value of system outputs. From that point of view, bulk buying of commodities such as food and clothing appears as a rational solution to the challenge of supporting a family of a given size from a given income. The challenge of producing a large number of children with only limited input from a small income would seem to necessitate careful attention to realizing such economies of scale.

In practice, it is unlikely that the economistic logic of production is the only, or even the most important, meaning given to householding in any family. As previously noted, the evidence for Canada indicates that decisions about clothes purchases for children are simply not made in that way. It is not hard to suggest why. In some of our contemporary "consumer societies," the clothing tastes of adults and children are so highly differentiated that a great deal of fuss is made about the uniqueness of each child. There is often considerable resistance to passing clothes on from one sibling to another. Even in the case of food, the tastes of each individual may be accorded such significance that the practical possibility of bulk buying for the entire family can be very small.

Sociologists need to pay more attention to analyzing the implicit assumptions that underlie economic models of families. Among other conditions, applying the logic of Fordist production to families seems to assume an ethic of unlimited sharing. It assumes that family members eat cooked meals together and that they are willing to share food out of the same pot. It also assumes that they will share personal items of clothing, sequentially if not simultaneously. These assumptions are probably less accurate guides to conduct now than they were in the past.

Instead of an ethic of unlimited sharing, it is more likely that individuals in post-Fordist families emphasize the costs of sharing. When things are shared, there must be compromises in aesthetic preferences at the point of purchase. People must also accept that shared things will wear out and get broken more quickly and that consumption will be limited to times when some other family member does not have priority access. None of this sounds very attractive to today's demanding consumers, adults or children.

The methodology of poverty analysis, narrowly conceived, has paid little attention to the costs of sharing. There is, however, a cognate field of social research in which it has been widely recognized. That field is housing studies.

In analyses of families and housing, it is generally understood that sharing the same space is likely to disrupt individuals' activities and that this can generate emotional stress. Although economies of scale can no doubt be achieved in housing production, the perspective of families as housing consumers is likely to be very different. Housing consumers typically prefer to have more than the legal minimum amount of space per person, and this is reflected in the social distribution of crowding.

Families with children are more crowded than families with no children in Canada and the United States. In Canada in 1992, the median number of persons per room recorded in the Family Expenditure Survey was 0.57 for households with children, but only 0.33 for households with no children. In the United States, the median number of persons per room in consumer units with no children was the same 0.33, but in consumer units with children it was a higher 0.67.

In both the United States and Canada, families with children make up the overwhelming majority of households with serious crowding problems. Families with children accounted for 75.9 percent of Canadian households in 1992 in which the number of persons per room was more than 50 percent above the national median. In the United States in that year, families with children comprised 80.6 percent of consumer units in which the number of persons per room was more than half as much again as the national average.

Finally, according to the conventional standard of overcrowding (i.e., one or more persons per room), 7.0 percent of Canadian families with children were overcrowded, compared with just 2.0 percent of families without children. Although only 2.6 percent of U.S. families without children were overcrowded in 1992, as many as 19.2 percent of families with children in the United States were overcrowded.

Analyses of poverty that rely on weighted measures of family income have tended to understate the difficulties of families with children, notably in housing. Arguably, the most serious result of this has been the neglect of inequalities *among* families with children. Children in small families and children in large families often have very different housing experiences.

When the first child is born, and as each additional child arrives, families meet their needs for increased living space by moving out of rented rooms and apartments and into single, detached houses, especially in Canada (see Table 5.1). Nevertheless, they are not always able to avoid crowding problems. Families with several children are generally more crowded, especially in the United States. In Canada, overcrowding is a problem only among families with three or more children. In the United States, overcrowding emerges as a minor problem in families with two children, but almost half of families with three or more children are overcrowded. Having several children is evidently a serious disadvantage in the U.S. housing market.

MORE CHILDREN, MORE POVERTY

In his study of York at the end of the nineteenth century, Seebohm Rowntree (1902) identified "largeness of family" as one of the principal causes of poverty. Family size was the third most important cause of poverty at the household level, but it had the second largest effect in terms of the number of poor persons. Big families obviously contain more people than small families. It is therefore the peculiar nature of this cause

TABLE 5.1

Dwelling Characteristics of Households in Canada and Consumer Units in the United States, by Number of Children Under Age 18

Dwelling Characteristics	Canada				United States			
	No Children	One Child	Two Children	Three or More Children	No Children	One Child	Two Children	Three or More Children
Home Ownership (Percent)	58.9	60.7	73.7	74.1	62.6	58.7	64.2	55.8
Type of Dwelling (Percent)								
Single House	49.2	56.3	69.9	75.5	58.7	64.0	71.8	68.5
Multiple–unit House	12.7	18.4	17.7	15.4	20.5	18.2	14.5	17.2
Apartment	34.9	22.6	10.6	6.6	12.2	9.7	7.5	9.5
Other	3.2	2.7	(1.8)	(2.5)	8.6	8.1	6.2	4.8
Number of Persons per Room (Median)	0.3	0.5	0.6	0.7	0.3	0.5	0.7	0.9
Overcrowding (Percent)	2.0	2.9	6.4	18.0	2.6	5.7	16.4	48.5

( ) Indicates cell is <30 cases.

of poverty that it affects a disproportionate number of individuals, and especially of children.

By "largeness of family" Rowntree meant families with more than four children, or, in other words, having five or more children. One of the most significant changes since Rowntree's initial study is that fertility rates have fallen considerably during this century. In the 1990s, there are very few families in any western society with five or more children. In fact, there are so few of them that they are usually not seen as having any noteworthy influence on the amount of poverty (Room, Lawson, & Laczko, 1989).

Although families with five or more children are no longer common, this does not necessarily mean that family size is an altogether irrelevant factor. Rather, it may mean that what counts as largeness of family has changed. As the average family size has shrunk, so the benchmark for a "large" family has fallen. Today, large families are those that have three or more children.

Income per Person

The incidence of poverty among families with children is heavily affected by the number of children in the family, especially when income is calculated per capita. On a per capita basis, families with three or more children in Canada and in the United States are approximately three times as likely as families with only one child to fall into the lowest net income decile (see Table 5.2). Large families are still the poorest families even when income per person is adjusted to give less weight to children than to adults. Based on reference equivalent, U.S. and Canadian families with three or more children are almost twice as likely to be in the lowest net income decile as are families with only one child.

We noted in Chapter 3 that income inequality is greater in the United States than it is in Canada. As a result, there are more poor families in the United States who have incomes far below the national median. That is especially true for poor families with children. Some of the figures on the depth of poverty in families with three or more children can only be described as alarming. Even when income is calculated per reference equivalent, two out of five large families in the United States have net incomes that are less than half the national average for consumer units. When net income is calculated per capita, well over half (57.3 percent) of U.S. families with three or more children have incomes less than half the national median. Almost half (47.8 percent) have per capita net incomes more than 60 percent below the national median.

Consistent with the findings on taxation regimes reported earlier, income taxes in the United States have little overall effect on either the rate or the depth of poverty among families with children. Also as expected, Canadian income tax deductions impose a relatively less onerous fiscal burden on poor families, thus decreasing the distance between their incomes and the national median income. However, Canadian taxation policy is no more likely than U.S. taxation policy to achieve a greater degree of distributive justice between families with different numbers of children. It is disturbing to note that families with three or more children in Canada are comparatively worse off in relation to other families with children after all taxes and government levies have been paid. Almost one-third (32.7 percent) of large Canadian families are in the bottom decile of per capita income before taxes. This rises to two-fifths (39.4 percent) of large families who are in the bottom decile of total money receipts per capita after all deductions.

Clothing

In large families, high demands are placed on available income. This affects how money is spent, and it affects who it is spent on.

One of the most clearly identifiable expenditure effects of the presence of children concerns the purchase of children's clothing. In the United States,[2] median annualized expenditure on clothes for children under age 16 increases from $272 in families with one child under age 16, through $424 in families with two children under age 16, to $515 in families with three or more children under age 16.[3]

Increased demand for children's clothing can be met in part by expanding the clothing envelope in the family's budget relative to other goods. In the United States, median total clothing expenditure is 3.9 percent of net income in one-child families. This increases to 4.4 percent of net income in families with three or more children. In Canada, clothes purchases as a proportion of money receipts after all deductions increase from 5.9 percent of available income in families with only one child to 6.8 percent of available income in families with three or more children.

In reality, the size of the clothing envelope does not change much as families grow in size. That is surely because children also need so many other things. Not only do children have to be housed and fed but they also need school supplies, they need toys and games equipment, they need

TABLE 5.2

Percentage of Households with Children in Canada and Consumer Units with Children in the United States in Income Poverty, by Number of Children Under Age 18

Income	One Child		Two Children		Three or More Children	
	Per Capita	Per Reference Equivalent	Per Capita	Per Reference Equivalent	Per Capita	Per Reference Equivalent
Lowest Decile						
Canada						
Income Before Taxes	12.3	9.4	17.5	9.1	32.7	15.0
Total Receipts After All Deductions	12.0	9.7	18.8	8.8	39.4	17.7
United States						
Income Before Taxes	13.1	12.6	14.9	10.5	36.5	20.9
Total Receipts After All Deductions	13.3	12.5	15.3	10.0	35.3	21.5
More Than 50 Percent Below Median						
Canada						
Income Before Taxes	14.8	13.4	20.5	14.1	37.3	21.8
Total Receipts After All Deductions	9.9	9.1	16.0	8.2	34.4	17.0

88

United States

Income Before Taxes	25.2	23.1	30.9	23.3	55.5	41.6
Total Receipts After All Deductions	25.1	22.0	33.5	22.4	57.3	39.8

More Than 60 Percent Below Median

Canada

Income Before Taxes	7.8	8.5	12.0	7.0	25.3	13.9
Total Receipts After All Deductions	3.5	2.7	7.6	3.4	20.4	7.2

United States

Income Before Taxes	20.4	18.0	23.2	16.1	48.4	31.9
Total Receipts After All Deductions	19.3	16.4	23.9	15.6	47.8	29.8

transportation, and so on. The major ways to meet increased demand for clothing in large families are, therefore, to press down on the costs of each family member and to re-allocate more of the clothing envelope for the children's use and less for the adults.

In families with children, the more children there are the greater is the proportion of the clothing envelope devoted to buying children's clothes, and conversely less is spent on adults' clothes (see Table 5.3). In this regard female sole parents appear to be particularly affected by the number of children in their care. Many sole-support mothers with large families in the United States must be among the most poorly clothed adults to be found anywhere in the postmodern world.

TABLE 5.3
Expenditure on Children's Clothing as a Percentage of Total Clothing Expenditure for Consumer Units with Children in the United States, by Family Type and Number of Children Under Age 16

Children's Clothing Expenditure	One or More Children	One Child	Two Children	Three or More Children
All Consumer Units	38.4	27.9	43.2	51.4
Married Couples	36.9	26.7	40.3	45.7
Female Sole Parents	44.6	31.5	64.7	61.4

Because of the sacrifices made by their mothers, children living in large families headed by a female sole parent do not fare quite as badly as we might expect. Nevertheless, they are clearly disadvantaged compared with other children. In two-parent families in the United States, the median expenditure on children's clothing per child falls from $314 in a family with one child, through $227 in a family with two children, to $159 in a family with three or more children. In families headed by a female sole parent, the median expenditure on children's clothing per child is $220 in a one-child family, $168 in a two-child family, and $125 in a family with three or more children. Clearly, some children are poorer than others. A child living in the United States in a large family headed by a sole-support mother has less than half of the money for clothes as a single child who is supported by both parents.

POOR CHILDREN

Children's lives are evidently greatly affected by the sizes of the families to which they belong. The significance of this fact for children is not always sufficiently understood. One reason for this is that data on poverty are usually presented, as they have been here, for the family rather than the individual child as the unit of analysis. When the family is taken as the unit of analysis, each family is counted as one unit regardless of how many children it contains. Families with only one child thus have the same weight as families with many children. The result is that the prevalence of children from large families appears to be understated. This point can be illustrated by showing that families with three or more children in the United States comprise only 22 percent of consumer units with children, yet they contain 40 percent of all children.

In the United States and in Canada, families with three or more children account for between one-fourth and two-fifths of all poor families with children, depending on how the calculations are made. However, the children from these large families comprise between one-half and two-thirds of the poorest children.

In Canada, families with three or more children contain 32 percent of all children, yet these children constitute 47.4 percent of children in the lowest decile of household net income calculated per reference equivalent and 52.7 percent calculated per capita. The figures for the United States are more extreme, in part because there are more large families in that country. Large families, which contain 40 percent of all U.S. children, are the source of 60.1 percent of children in the lowest decile of consumer unit net income per reference equivalent and 64.5 percent if net income is calculated per capita. From a child's point of view, poverty is above all a shared experience among siblings.

DISCUSSION

This chapter has shown that child poverty, which was a serious problem at the end of the nineteenth century, is still a problem today. It has also been shown that contemporary analyses of the extent and causes of the problem are complicated by the expanded role of governments over the past hundred years. Governments are now involved in the collection of social statistics on poverty, and they administer taxation and transfer programs that affect the incomes of the poor. The connections between these two sets of activities have fateful consequences for families with several children. These families are greatly impacted by the ways in which poverty statistics are analyzed and presented.

The poverty of children who live in families that are larger than the norm for their society has not been solved in North America in the twentieth century. Normal family size has fallen as women have reduced their fertility, but the families that deviate from the norm by having "too many" children remain on the margins. Family size declined during the twentieth century, most notably after the baby boom that followed the end of World War II. The majority of families in the United States and Canada today contain only one or two children. We might have thought, then, that family size had ceased to be a significant determinant of poverty by the last decade of the twentieth century. If we thought that, we would have been wrong.

The analysis of marital status in the previous chapter showed how changes in family composition that occurred since the beginning of the twentieth century brought about a significant shift in the social distribution of poverty. In contrast, we have seen in this chapter that the causation of children's poverty by family size exhibits a remarkable continuity (although admittedly the definition of what is meant by a "large" family has to be adjusted downward).

It is important to note that poverty in large families is not due mainly to such families being socially disorganized or irresponsible. For instance, their poverty cannot be explained by sole-support mothers having more children than married mothers because, on average, they do not.

In the United States in 1992, consumer units containing a married couple and children had an average (mean) of 2.0 children, as did consumer units with a single (i.e., never married) mother as reference person. If the reference person was a separated mother, the average number of co-resident children was 2.2. When the reference person was a divorced mother the average was 1.8, and when the reference person was a widowed mother the average was 1.7. In Canada in 1992, households consisting of a married couple and children contained 1.8 children on average. Households headed by single mothers had an average of 1.4 children, and households headed by separated, divorced, or widowed mothers had an average of 1.7 children. There is no evidence here of poverty in large families due to irresponsible reproduction by solo mothers.

It is sometimes suggested that there exists an underclass of chronic welfare recipients, many of whom are female sole parents, who realize that they can get more welfare benefits by having more children and who therefore increase their fertility. Assuming that this is true might help to account for the greater prevalence of large families among the poor. If this hypothesis is correct, then we should find that families on welfare have more children than those who are not on welfare. There is some modest supporting evidence for this in the United States, but the evidence in Canada is only weak.

We can look at this issue by comparing families who receive welfare and those who do not, for married couples and for female sole parents. In Canada, married couples not on welfare have an average (mean) of 1.8 children living at home, and married couples who receive welfare have an almost identical average of 1.9 children. Canadian female sole parents on average have 1.5 co-resident children if they are not on welfare and an average of 1.8 children if they are welfare recipients.

In the United States, female sole parents have 1.7 children if they do not receive welfare but 2.4 children if they do. Similarly, married couples have 1.9 children if they are not on welfare and 2.7 children if they are welfare recipients.

In light of the difference between the United States and Canada in the relationship between welfare dependence and fertility, it is relevant to note that a prominent factor in discussions of this topic in the United States is race (Jencks, 1991). Perhaps black welfare mothers have more children than white mothers. In practice, there is no difference in fertility patterns between blacks and whites in the United States that could account for the greater poverty of larger families. Among families with children who do not receive welfare, whites have an average of 1.9 children per family and blacks have an average of 2.0 children per family. In families with children supported by welfare, blacks have an average of 2.6 children and whites have an average of 2.3 children.

It is interesting to speculate on alternative explanations for the higher average number of children among families on welfare in the United States, compared to Canada. Possibly, the low levels of minimum wages in many states, together with difficulties in obtaining health insurance, make welfare relatively more attractive as an economic base for large working-class families in the United States.

Most parents of large families are not work-shy. In Canada, 83.1 percent of reference persons for households with one child were employed at some time in 1992, as were 86.3 percent of reference persons for households with two children and 81.0 percent of reference persons for households with three or more children. In the United States, 85.6 percent of reference persons were engaged in some employment in both one-child and two-child families, while in families with three or more children 75.8 percent of reference persons were employed.

The first point to note about these figures is that they show that between three-fourths and four-fifths of the individuals who have the primary responsibility for economic provision for a family of three or more children are employed in North America in a given year. That is not much below the rate of employment for reference persons in families with one or two children. The second point to note is what these figures do not show. They do not show the overwhelming extent to which married men are committed to working to support the children in their families, regardless of family size. In two-parent families of all types, more than nine-tenths of social fathers are employed for a part or all of the year. In the United States, the rate of employment of social fathers is 92.3 percent in one-child families, 94.5 percent in two-child families, and 91.5 percent in families with three or more children. In Canada, the rate of employment of social fathers is 91.8 percent in families with one child, 95.7 percent in families with two children, and 93.8 percent in families with three or more children. It does not appear that there are many residential fathers who avoid the duty to work and who, instead, rely upon the state to support them and their children.

It is, of course, true that in the second half of the twentieth century there was a great expansion of the welfare state. In principle, one of the tasks of the welfare state is to provide public subsidies for the private costs of reproduction, so that less than the full weight of providing for children falls on those who are unable to bear it. Certainly, major efforts were made in this direction from the late 1940s through the 1970s. However, in recent years this movement has lost headway, and in the 1990s more of the costs of childrearing are being shifted back onto families (Strawn, 1992; Battle, 1993).

Perhaps the most dramatic reversal of a longstanding commitment to provide public support for the private costs of reproduction was the gradual reduction in the universal Family Allowance program in Canada and its eventual elimination at the end of 1992 (Rice & Prince, 1993). In any event, government transfer payments have not raised all children out of poverty, and the income taxation systems in Canada and the United States have not lessened the marginalization of children in large families.

Despite all the changes that occurred during the twentieth century, the poverty of children in large families has the same source today as it did a century ago, when it was first described in England by Rowntree. Families with an above-average number of young children are often poor, because the combined efforts of the family members cannot produce enough income to support all of them at a reasonable standard of living.

NOTES

1.   The differential impact of families with children on the reported distribution of poverty according to whether income is adjusted per capita or per reference equivalent is due to the fact that weighted family size adjustments tend to increase the visibility of poverty in single-person units, whereas per capita family size adjustments tend to increase the visibility of poverty in multiperson units.

2.   Expenditures on children's clothing could not be calculated for Canadian families of different compositions, because the age categories for household members employed in the 1992 Family Expenditure Survey public use file do not correspond with the age cut-off used for recording children's clothing.

3.   Median annualized expenditure on children's clothing per child under age 16 in the United States falls from $272 in families with one child under age 16, through $212 in families with two children under age 16, to $148 in families with three or more children under age 16. The sharp decline in clothing expenditure per child in large families in the United States is most likely due to the extreme pressure on the householding budget in these families, as a result of their very low per capita incomes (see Table 5.2).

6

Family Work Systems

During the twentieth century, the social organization of work changed
considerably. On the one hand, employers constantly changed the demand
for different types of work and the financial rewards paid. As the shifting
of the demand for labor accelerated toward the end of the twentieth century, this process came to be known as "economic restructuring." On the
other hand, families altered the supply of labor. They changed the manner
in which family members' labor is allocated between internal domestic
services and employment for wages. As they did so, the family economy
was recomposed.

The family economy (Elder, 1977), or household economy (Wilk,
1989), consists of organized practices through which members of a family
meet their individual and collective needs. One set of practices involves
the allocation of human labor, or work, to different tasks. This often takes
the form of a division of labor between family members, who engage in
work of different kinds. In traditional breadwinner-homemaker families,
for example, the husband goes out to work to earn the family wage while
the wife maintains the home and looks after any children or other family
members in need of care.

In the nineteenth century, one earnings strategy that was widely
employed by working-class families was to send children out to work as
soon as possible. Rowntree (1902) reported that in York at the end of the
nineteenth century the wages of older children often played an important

role in lifting large families out of poverty. However, the relative value of children's unskilled labor declined as industrialization advanced. Furthermore, great importance came to be attached to prolonged schooling for children as a way of fostering upward social mobility. As a result, children were gradually withdrawn from the labor market, and married women's employment was substituted for the work of their children (Oppenheimer, 1994).

The flexibility of wives' employment came to be a highly adaptive strategy to cope with fluctuations in the family's need for money. Married women's work outside the home increased gradually throughout the first four decades of the twentieth century, but it increased sharply after 1940. In the United States, almost 70 percent of wives between the ages of 20 and 54 were in the labor force by 1990, compared with less than 20 percent in 1940 and only about 5 percent in 1900 (Oppenheimer, 1994, p. 297). The pattern of change in Canada was similar. In 1931 only 3.5 percent of Canadian married women were employed, but by the 1980s more than half of all wives were employed (McDaniel, 1988).

An important consequence of the increased employment of wives has been a large growth in the number of dual-earner families (Rubin & Riney, 1994). Dual-earner families have undergone a remarkable transition, from minority to majority lifestyle among husband-wife families active in the labor market. In the 1960s, the dominant family type was still the traditional breadwinner-homemaker family, containing a married heterosexual couple in which only the husband was employed. Today the dominant family type is the double-income family, in which both spouses are in the labor force (Statistics Canada, 1992). This transition can be illustrated for Canada by comparing the beginning and end of the twenty-year period 1967–86 (Moore, 1989, p. 24). In 1967, traditional breadwinner-homemaker families comprised 61 percent of husband-wife families active in the labor market, whereas dual-earner families constituted only 34 percent. Twenty years later the situation had been reversed. In 1986, dual-earner families comprised 62 percent of husband-wife families active in the labor market, and the relative frequency of traditional breadwinner-homemaker families had fallen to 27 percent. Dramatic as these figures are, they understate the economic and social significance of double-income families in Canada today since they ignore the effects of generational change. In 1986, 74 percent of families in which the husband was under age 45 had two earners (Moore, 1989, p. 25). Dual-earner families have therefore sometimes been described as "the new norm" for husband-wife families.

There are two important exceptions to the narrative of dual-earner families as the emergent norm in contemporary societies. We have already noted that sole-parent families, too, have increased in frequency in recent years (Hudson & Galaway, 1993). These families sometimes join with other families in complex households, in which there may be two or more adult earners. In families headed by older female sole parents, the wages of adult children can make important contributions to the household economy (Rashid, 1994). Nevertheless, for the many female sole parents who live alone with their minor children, the economic reality is very simple. There can be at most only one income earner in these households.

The second important exception to the trend toward more work-intensive dual-earner families is the existence of large numbers of unattached individuals, especially among young adults. In Canada, the proportion of never-married singles has been increasing in all age groups under 45, as people are tending to marry at later ages (Devereaux, 1990). By 1992, the average age at first marriage in Canada was 29 for men and 27 for women (Oderkirk, 1994). This had increased by four years since the 1960s, when average age at first marriage had been 25 for men and 23 for women.

Many young unattached adults continue to live at home with their parents, especially at younger ages and especially if they are still in school (Boyd & Pryor, 1989). However, by their late twenties the clear majority of unattached men and women are living independently, many of them in one-person households. These single adults are economically vulnerable in hard times. From the early 1980s to the early 1990s there was a moderate but steady increase in the incidence of poverty among them (Ross, Shillington, & Lochhead, 1994).

INCOME EARNING

In the present chapter we will examine some of the economic consequences of the number of earners in the household. This involves taking into account not only the social composition of the household or consumer unit but also the social distribution of employment and unemployment. Furthermore, having one or more employed persons in a household does not in itself guarantee that the members will avoid poverty. The quantity of work performed, in terms of the number of hours per week and weeks per year, also strongly affects the amount of income derived from employment (Zill & Nord, 1994; Crompton, 1995), as does the rate of pay (Picot, Myles, & Wannell, 1990).

The material well-being of most families depends upon some variable combination of the number of members employed for wages, the amount of work performed, and the rate of pay. These three dimensions of the relationship between the household economy and the labor market are therefore very important factors in the production of poverty. How much effect does each of them have on poverty? Are there any patterns in the familial distribution of wage labor that are associated with being poor in North America at the end of the twentieth century?

At the end of the nineteenth century, Rowntree (1902) analyzed separately the three dimensions of the relationship between the household economy and the labor market, and their effects on the risk of being poor. He found the most common condition of poverty to be when the man, who was the chief wage-earner, was regularly employed, but his wages were insufficient to maintain a family of moderate size. This condition was responsible for 87.8 percent of the households that were poor for purely economic reasons. The next most important economic factor was irregularity of work by the main income provider. This accounted for 7.0 percent of the poverty arising from difficulties in relation to the labor market. Last, only 5.2 percent of economically induced poverty was a result of unemployment of the chief wage-earner.[1]

In late twentieth-century North America, the person providing the main financial support must still be employed full-time at high or medium wages if a household is to have only a small risk of being poor. The three factors of low wages, underemployment, and unemployment continue to be important causes of poverty in North America. However, their effects are not felt in the same way as described by Rowntree. The relative importance of these factors has generally been reversed (see Table 6.1).

In the United States and Canada in the early 1990s, the relative impact of the level of wages earned by the chief wage-earner was much less than that which existed in York almost a century before. At most, only one-fifth of nonelderly households in the lowest decile of net income in both countries were poor because the reference person was a full-year worker[2] who earned low wages.[3] Less than one-seventh of low-income poverty among the nonelderly was a result of regularly employed male family heads earning low wages.

The disparity between Rowntree's description of the poor at the end of the nineteenth century and the picture presented in Table 6.1 is a forceful reminder of the need for theories of poverty that take into account the changes that occurred in the second half of the twentieth century. There appear to be three main reasons why a low wage of a male breadwinner is

TABLE 6.1
Distribution of Poverty in Canada and the United States, by Employment Activity and Gender of Reference Person. Percentage of Households and Consumer Units with Reference Person Under Age 65 in Lowest Decile of Total Receipts After All Deductions

Reference Person	Not Employed		Part-Year Work		Full-Year Work, Low Wages		Full-Year Work, Medium Wages		Full-Year Work, High Wages	
	Per Capita	Per Reference Equivalent	Per Capita	Per Reference Equivalent	Per Capita	Per Reference Equivalent	Per Capita	Per Reference Equivalent	Per Capita	Per Reference Equivalent
Canada										
Male	17.2	23.9	15.2	10.4	13.0	7.0	3.9	0	(0.3)	(0.2)
Female	30.7	39.3	15.6	15.8	4.0	(3.4)	(0.1)	0	0	0
All	47.9	63.2	30.8	26.2	17.0	10.4	4.0	0	(0.3)	(0.2)
United States										
Male	11.6	12.1	16.6	21.1	13.3	10.8	(3.0)	(0.2)	(0.8)	(0.6)
Female	31.6	30.2	16.0	20.5	(7.1)	(4.5)	0	0	0	0
All	43.2	42.3	32.6	41.6	20.4	15.3	(3.0)	(0.2)	(0.8)	(0.6)

( ) Indicates cell is <30 cases.

no longer the major determinant of household poverty. The reasons are the restructuring of work and employment, the increased importance of women as economic actors, and the growing complexity and diversification of household economies. Brief remarks will be made about each of these factors in turn.

Restructuring of Work and Employment

Among North American families as a whole, absence of regular employment by the reference person is the principal economic cause of low household income today, followed by working for only part of the year. The least important economic cause of poverty is low wages earned by the reference person, regardless of gender. Not surprisingly, the politics of poverty has changed in North America in recent years as it has increasingly focused on the nonworking poor (Mead, 1992).

Lack of full-year employment is somewhat more serious among men in Canada than it is in the United States, as we would expect from the higher Canadian rate of unemployment.[4] In contrast, among U.S. men it is working less than full-time that appears to be the most common cause of poverty. Those differences aside, when incomes are adjusted per capita the economic causes of low income have similar overall effects in the United States and in Canada. (Adjusting incomes per reference equivalent produces more variation, presumably due to demographic differences).

In recent decades, the financial well-being of families in North America has been adversely affected by broad international developments in labor markets and in occupational practices (Voydanoff, 1990). Unemployment became a major problem in most western nations from the mid-1970s through the 1990s, as companies adjusted to intensified competition (Gaffikin & Morrissey, 1992). Jobs were lost due to corporate downsizing, and new job creation often failed to keep pace with the demand for paid work. At the same time, the mix of available positions shifted (Ternowetsky & Thorn, 1991). Employers placed a greater emphasis on the increased flexibility of labor and on reducing the costs incurred by the benefits provided for full-time employees. In particular, there was a growing concentration of part-time work in service occupations (Jacobs, 1993). The overall result has been greater casualization of work, with more people working part-time or for only part of the year.

Economic Emergence of Women

A shortage of hours of paid work has been a general problem in North America in recent years. However, not being employed is a particularly prevalent cause of poverty when women are responsible for maintaining a household.

In the majority of households containing adults of both sexes, the senior male is usually identified as the person with the largest income and the most property, the person who provides the main economic support. Nevertheless, women are increasingly active as autonomous economic agents who mediate their families' relationships with business corporations and government agencies. That is especially so when women form independent households without a male partner. In the 1992 U.S. and Canadian expenditure surveys, 36.6 percent of U.S. consumer units were designated as having a female reference person, as were 42.2 percent of Canadian households.

The relative unimportance of low-wage-earning male family heads in the contemporary social distribution of poverty, which was noted earlier, can be partly attributed to the feminization of poverty among the nonelderly. More than half of poor households and consumer units in Canada and the United States are supported by women now. In Canada in 1992, female-headed households comprised 50.4 percent of nonelderly households falling in the lowest decile of net income per capita and 58.5 percent when net income is calculated per reference equivalent. In the United States, consumer units headed by a woman accounted for 54.7 percent of nonelderly units in the lowest decile of per capita incomes in 1992 and 55.2 percent of consumer units in the lowest decile of incomes per reference equivalent.

Recently, a great deal of attention has been paid to the fact that employed women's earnings continue to be lower than men's earnings for comparable work. In the United States in 1992, women working full-time earned 71 percent as much as men (Farley, 1994). The situation in Canada is almost identical. In 1991, Canadian women working full-time and full-year earned on average 70 percent as much as comparable men (Ghalam, 1993). We might therefore expect that the lower wages of regularly employed women would be a significant cause of poverty in female-headed families. However, that is not the case. In both Canada and the United States, low wages earned by women in full-year work are directly responsible for only about 4 percent of nonelderly families in the lowest decile of net income. The largest cause by far of poverty in female-headed families is simply that the reference person is not employed.

Female reference persons are much less likely to be employed than male reference persons. According to the U.S. Consumer Expenditure Survey, 9.2 percent of male reference persons under age 65 were not employed in 1992, whereas 24.8 percent of female reference persons were not employed. In Canada, 13.3 percent of male reference persons were not employed, compared with 28.3 percent of female reference persons.

Pluralism of Family Systems

Differences in employment characteristics between households in which women or men are the main income generators are important aspects of the pluralism of contemporary family systems. Living arrangements and family lifestyles have become increasingly diverse. This process, which Hughes (1991) refers to as *household diversification*, includes greater variation in the ways in which households mobilize and manage their resources.

Families today engage in a variety of work and income-generating practices. Current patterns of household formation continue to shift away from the traditional nuclear family, and we need to pay careful attention to the economic implications of this change (Morris, 1995). Doyle (1985) believes that this shift is producing an increasing number of people, such as female sole parents, who, by the nature of their living arrangements, are more vulnerable to financial problems.

The greater economic difficulties of families led by women are not due only to their lower level of participation in the labor force. Even when male and female reference persons are both out of work, it is still the case that female-headed households are worse off, notably in the United States. One explanation for this pattern is that female reference persons are much more likely to be unmarried than male reference persons, and especially so in the United States.[5] Women who maintain households but who are not employed, and who are also without husbands, do not have a partner's income as a cushion against deprivation. Not being employed has a bigger negative impact on the financial resources available to these women than it has on married individuals.

The interaction between the effect of marital status and the effect of employment activity on the risk of poverty is a classic illustration of the point that an individual's chance of being poor does not depend entirely on his or her personal earning power. It also depends on the role that money plays in relation to other sources of income in the structure of the household economy.

LINKED LIVES

Households are fundamental economic units, because within them financial resources are pooled as "family money" to achieve collective purposes. Pooling is especially characteristic of marriage partners. Blumstein and Schwartz (1983) report from a large survey in the United States that a majority of couples assume when they marry that they should pool all of their property and financial assets. The moral economy of marriage deserves more attention in sociological studies of poverty, because sharing between partners provides some protection against economic deprivation for individuals with low or nil earnings.

Sgritta observes that the study of the family's "composite income" has become necessary, in light of the crisis of the welfare state. He argues that the composite income produced by a family "assumes the job of compensating for that part of social demand for goods and services which the state and the market cannot provide or are no longer able to supply" (1989, p. 82).

Pooling is an important aspect of family life, because different members may contribute different kinds and amounts of resources to the household economy, and because some members are highly dependent upon financial contributions from others. That is usually the case in relations between parents and young children, and it often happens in relations between husbands and wives as well. Although the practical extent of income sharing varies greatly (Cheal, 1993b), wage pooling is generally considered to be essential to the functioning of families and to be related to positive family characteristics such as marital satisfaction and involvement with children (Friedman, 1984; Coleman & Ganong, 1989; Wilk, 1989).

The following working hypotheses can be proposed concerning personal resources and marital pooling, and their relation to the risk of poverty.

1. Households that are supported by an individual who has few personal resources are more likely to be poor than households that are supported by an individual who has greater personal resources.

2. Households that are supported by an unmarried person are more likely to be poor than households that are supported by a husband and wife together. Low personal resources of one partner can often be supplemented if the other partner possesses more personal resources.

3. Since women generally have fewer personal resources than men, it follows from 1 and 2 above that households that are supported by

unmarried women are very likely to be poor.

4. In households that are supported by married couples, the probability of being poor will be a function of the combined resources of the partners.

5. It follows from 1 and 4 above that households that are supported by partners who are both lacking in resources are likely to be poor.

Patterns of economic life chances can be illustrated for unmarried individuals and married couples in Canadian households and U.S. consumer units having reference persons under age 65 whose total money receipts after all deductions per capita lie in the bottom quintile of the income distribution. (The bottom quintile, rather than the usual bottom decile, will be used to identify the income poor in this chapter because it is necessary to have a large number of cases in order to report accurately on a range of subgroups among the poor.) For both countries, 12 main types of domestic units can be identified that contain most of the nonelderly poor. They are listed, in descending order of relative frequency among the poor in each country.

United States	*Consumer Units in Lowest Quintile of Net Income*
11.5%	Separated, divorced, or widowed woman, not employed
7.5%	Separated, divorced, or widowed woman, part-year wage worker
7.2%	Never-married woman, part-year wage worker
7.0%	Never-married man, part-year wage worker
6.4%	Never-married woman, not employed
6.0%	Couple, husband full-year wage worker at low wage and wife not employed
5.8%	Couple, husband and wife both not employed
5.7%	Couple, husband part-year wage worker and wife not employed
5.0%	Couple, husband full-year wage worker at medium wage and wife not employed
4.7%	Couple, husband full-year wage worker at low wage and wife part-year wage worker
4.2%	Separated, divorced, or widowed woman, full-year wage worker at low wage
3.8%	Couple, husband and wife both part-year wage workers

74.8%

Canada	*Households in Lowest Quintile of Net Income*
11.3%	Separated, divorced, or widowed woman, not employed
10.5%	Couple, husband and wife both not employed
9.6%	Couple, husband part-year wage worker and wife not employed

Canada	Households in Lowest Quintile of Net Income
8.9%	Couple, husband and wife both part-year wage workers
6.7%	Couple, husband full-year wage worker at low wage and wife part-year wage worker
6.3%	Couple, husband full-year wage worker at medium wage and wife not employed
5.7%	Never-married woman not employed
5.7%	Separated, divorced, or widowed woman part-year wage worker
5.6%	Couple, husband full-year wage worker at low wage and wife not employed
4.3%	Couple, husband full-year wage worker at medium wage and wife part-year wage worker
3.3%	Couple, husband and wife both full-year wage worker at low wages
3.2%	Never-married woman part-year wage worker

81.1%

The examples presented above confirm what was reported earlier about the economic causes of poverty, namely, that the level of individual wages is not the principal determinant of poverty in the 1990s. Absence of employment and partial employment are more conspicuous features of the relationship between poor households and the labor market than low earnings. Even among women, whose lesser earnings might be thought to predispose them to low-wage poverty, it is lack of work rather than wage inequality that accounts for most poverty.

Data concerning personal earning power and marital status also show something else very important about the economic circumstances of the poor. Poverty is found mainly in households in which individuals who do not have significant market incomes also do not have strong family financial supports. Such individuals have little informal protection against the risks of the labor market. As a result, they tend to be overrepresented among the poor.

ON THEIR OWN

Unmarried individuals who do not have a spouse to help support them make up a growing proportion of the poor in North America. In Canada, 35.2 percent of nonelderly households in the bottom quintile of net income per capita have an unmarried individual as the reference person. That is slightly higher than the percentage of all such households in the population, at 32.7 percent. In the United States, 55.5 percent of non-elderly consumer units with low per capita incomes are maintained by an unmarried individual, which is well above the 43.4 percent of all non-elderly consumer units with that domestic arrangement.

When household (or consumer unit) incomes are adjusted using Statistics Canada's equivalence scale, the domestic units of unmarried reference persons are greatly overrepresented among the poor. In Canada, 56.4 percent of households in the bottom quintile of net income per reference equivalent contain an unmarried reference person. In the United States, the reference person is unmarried in 68.1 percent of nonelderly households with net income per reference equivalent in the bottom quintile.

Some unmarried individuals are less likely to fall into poverty than others when the economy is bad. Individuals who are separated, divorced, or widowed may receive unearned income, such as alimony or child support payments, life insurance policies, and interest on personal savings or investments acquired through property division or inheritance. On the other hand, people who were never married are unlikely to have significant unearned incomes. They do not have any residual property rights from marriage and, because they are generally younger, they are likely to have only modest savings. Lack of earnings, and therefore lack of employment, have an immediate impact on never-married persons, especially if they are living alone as single adults.[6] With very little money and few or no relatives or other social supports to turn to, many poor single people are at high risk of homelessness. The circumstances of these individuals are of particular importance for understanding the growth of homelessness in the U.S. population, because almost three-fourths of homeless households consist of a single man and another tenth consist of a single woman (Burt, 1992).

In a labor market that does not supply enough work to meet all of the demand for paid employment, never-married individuals living on their own are economically vulnerable. As a result, single adults are more likely than married couples to be living in poverty (See Table 6.2).

In certain respects, single adults occupy a uniquely favorable position in the contemporary political economy of capitalism. They have the highest educational levels of any demographic group. For example, in Canada 20.4 percent of single adults under age 65 have a university degree, compared with 16.6 percent of nonelderly husbands and 12.0 percent of nonelderly wives. In the United States, 37.7 percent of single adults under age 65 are college graduates, compared with 29.0 percent of

TABLE 6.2
Percentage of Married Couples and Single Adults in Poverty for Total Receipts After All Deductions, among Households and Consumer Units with Reference Person Under Age 65, in Canada and the United States

Total Receipts After All Deductions	Married		Single Adult	
	Per Capita	Per Reference Equivalent	Per Capita	Per Reference Equivalent
Canada				
Lowest Decile	10.5	5.5	12.8	21.7
Lowest Quintile	21.0	11.2	21.1	32.4
United States				
Lowest Decile	8.1	5.7	14.3	21.0
Lowest Quintile	18.2	11.6	25.2	31.5

husbands and 23.2 percent of wives. Furthermore, single adults are much less likely than married persons to be in those manual occupations that have been in decline in recent years, such as factory production, construction, mining, and machining. Nevertheless, single adults were much less likely than the married to be fully employed in the early 1990s. That was either because more of them were only partially employed (United States) or because more of them were not working at all (United States and Canada). Due to their younger average age, single adults are more recent entrants into the labor market.[7] They are therefore more affected by current hiring conditions. In the early 1990s, those conditions were not favorable for full-time, full-year employment, and single adults suffered as a result.

In the nonelderly population in the United States in 1992, 14.1 percent of single adults were not employed, 35.7 percent of single adults were partially employed, and 50.2 percent of single adults were fully employed. Among married reference persons, 11.7 percent were not employed, 19.5 percent were partially employed, and 68.8 percent were fully employed. For Canadians under age 65 the pattern is similar (although more married persons in Canada than in the United States are only partially employed, and more single Canadians are not working). In Canada, 24.7 percent of single adults were not employed, 26.5 percent were partially employed, and 48.8 percent were fully employed. For married reference persons in

Canada, 15.6 percent were not employed, 29.3 percent were partially employed, and 55.1 percent were fully employed.

Because single adults are younger than married couples, it is possible that the lesser employment of the former may be due to the fact that more of them are attending college and are therefore not available for full-time employment. In the United States, 4.9 percent of married reference persons and 26.7 percent of single adult reference persons under age 65 were currently attending college at the time of interview in 1992. (All figures here are for the United States, because current educational participation is not available from the Canadian Family Expenditure Survey).

When reference persons currently attending college are removed from the U.S. Consumer Expenditure Survey sample, the labor force participation of single adults increases relative to the married, but most of the difference between the two groups remains. In the nonelderly, noncollege population in the United States in 1992, 15.8 percent of single adults were not employed, 28.1 percent of single adults were partially employed, and 56.1 percent of single adults were fully employed. The employment prospects of working-age single adults not attending college were less secure in the early 1990s than those of their married counterparts.

Single adults stand on their own, and their fortunes therefore rise and fall with the state of the labor market. Single adults are no more likely than husbands or wives to be poor when they are fully employed. However, the poverty rate of single adults is much higher than that of the married when they are not employed (see Table 6.3). When they are fully employed, single adults do not seem to have any less earning power to keep themselves out of poverty than do married individuals; the never-married who are living alone have much greater difficulty in managing the economic consequences of being out of work than do co-resident married couples.

MARRIAGE AND PROTECTION AGAINST POVERTY

Compared with single adults, married couples who pool their incomes are often able to protect themselves from the worst effects of lack of employment. In particular, couples in which both partners are involved in the labor force have more economic resilience than single individuals. The importance of this point can be illustrated from the U.S. recession of the early 1980s. The effects on families of an unprecedented level of unemployment were moderated by the presence of a second earner in two-thirds of the families affected by a job loss (Rubin & Riney, 1994). This provided a major cushion against the effects of unemployment on family income.

If married couples have enjoyed partial protection from the effects of failing labor markets in North America, the nature of that protection should be clarified. A simple comparison of poverty rates between the single and the married oversimplifies the true picture of that protection, because it ignores the fact that husbands and wives often relate to the labor market in different ways. In the United States, 73.9 percent of husbands under age 65 were fully employed in 1992, but only 37.8 percent of nonelderly wives were fully employed. In Canada, 63.5 percent of nonelderly husbands were fully employed, and just 34.0 percent of wives were fully employed. One result of this employment pattern is that wives have received more protection from poverty than husbands.

A nonworking wife under age 65 is more likely to have a fully employed husband (51.6 percent in Canada, 66.0 percent in the United States), than a nonworking husband under age 65 is to have a fully employed wife (18.5 percent in Canada, 22.5 percent in the United States). Similarly, a fully employed wife is more likely to have a fully employed husband (80.2 percent in the United States, 71.7 percent in Canada), than a fully employed husband is to have a fully employed wife (41.0 percent in the United States, 38.4 percent in Canada). Since husbands are more likely to be fully employed than wives, and because husbands' incomes are generally larger than wives' incomes, wives' contributions to the family economy are less likely to influence the family's risk of poverty than their husbands' contributions. In each category of labor force participation (i.e., nonworking, partially employed, fully employed), the incidence of poverty in wives' families is less than that in husbands' families (see Table 6.3). Marriage therefore provides more protection against poverty for wives than it does for husbands.

DISCUSSION

We have found in this chapter that there are complex interactions between labor market participation, marital status, and the risk of poverty within contemporary family work systems. The principal market causes of low household income today are lack of regular employment and working for only part of the year. However, poverty is found mainly in households in which individuals who do not have significant market incomes also do

TABLE 6.3

Percentage in Poverty for Total Receipts After All Deductions among Households and Consumer Units with Reference Person Under Age 65, by Single Adults' and Married Couples' Labor Force Participation, in Canada and the United States

Total Receipts After All Deductions	Nonworking		Partially Employed		Fully Employed	
	Per Capita	Per Reference Equivalent	Per Capita	Per Reference Equivalent	Per Capita	Per Reference Equivalent
Canada						
Lowest Decile						
Singles	36.1	58.5	(12.1)	22.3	(1.4)	(2.8)
Wives	21.4	13.5	8.8	3.4	3.4	(1.2)
Husbands	26.6	21.9	14.6	6.6	5.9	2.0
Lowest Quintile						
Singles	57.9	78.8	21.7	34.0	(2.2)	8.1
Wives	38.0	24.3	20.2	8.5	8.0	3.3
Husbands	40.0	33.6	27.7	15.2	14.9	5.4

United States						
Lowest Decile						
Singles	59.3	55.7	15.6	33.8	(2.0)	(2.7)
Wives	18.7	14.4	5.8	(3.2)	(2.0)	(1.5)
Husbands	27.4	21.2	9.8	(7.9)	5.3	3.3
Lowest Quintile						
Singles	70.8	77.9	38.2	50.9	(4.1)	(5.3)
Wives	34.1	24.7	17.2	9.5	7.1	(3.0)
Husbands	45.4	39.4	25.3	14.3	13.2	7.2

( ) Indicates cell is <30 cases.

not have strong family financial supports. Never-married individuals living on their own are especially likely to be poor. In contrast to single adults, marriage partners often have the ability to protect each other from poverty due to lack of employment. Recognition of the effects that family work systems have on the incidence of poverty requires a reorientation of social analysis away from the modernist preoccupation with markets and states and toward a broader conceptualization of the determinants of life chances.

In an explicit attempt at reviving commitment to the idea of progress, Ralf Dahrendorf (1979) has argued for the necessity of reconstructing the concept of life chances in sociological theory (see also van Kempen, 1994). Life chances are opportunities for individual development that are provided by social structures. Dahrendorf states that opportunities are provided in two ways. He refers to these different dimensions of opportunity as options (or choices) and ligatures (or linkages). In the former case, opportunities are provided as individual freedoms to choose between different lines of action (e.g., due to the possession of a personal income). In the latter case, opportunities are provided in the form of transactions between people who share social ties. These ties often involve restrictions on individual choice, but they provide access to opportunities that would not otherwise exist, such as access to a partner's income within the bonds of marriage.

In the present chapter we have seen how the presence of social linkages in marriage can provide a barrier against poverty. In the next chapter we will see how marriage can also increase the risk of poverty for some people.

NOTES

1.   Rowntree noted that unemployment was low in York at the time of his study, due to "an almost unexampled demand for labour" in the summer of 1899 (Rowntree, 1902, p. 125). Rowntree's report is, therefore, not necessarily typical of the experience of all cities at the end of the nineteenth century, over the full term of the capitalist cycle of boom and bust.

2.   The following definitions of employment categories were used for this study. "Full-year" refers to working more than 48 full-time equivalent weeks in the past year. "Part-year" refers to working more than two full-time equivalent weeks but not a full year. Not employed refers to working only two full-time equivalent weeks or less in the past year. The number of full-time equivalent weeks worked is the number of weeks worked full-time, plus the number of part-time weeks divided by two.

3.   In order to have a uniform basis for the cross-national analysis of personal income data, low wages were defined as incomes falling within the bottom three deciles of income before taxes of household or consumer unit reference persons under age 65 who were full-year workers. Medium wages were defined as incomes within the middle four deciles. High wages were defined as lying within the top three deciles. All data analyzed in this chapter are for households or consumer units with reference persons under age 65, since the elderly tend to have significantly different work and earning patterns associated with retirement.

4.   The relative frequencies of employment activity of different kinds among reference persons under age 65, as reported in the 1992 Canadian Family Expenditure Survey and the 1992 U.S. Consumer Expenditure Survey, are as follows. Canada: full-year work = 51.7 percent; part-year work = 28.9 percent; not employed = 19.4 percent. United States: full-year work = 61.9 percent; part-year work = 23.5 percent; not employed = 14.6 percent. There is a difference of ten percentage points in the total number of reference persons employed full-year in the two countries. About half of this difference is due to higher Canadian unemployment, and the other half is due to greater underemployment in Canada. The family work systems of married couples in the two countries show smaller differences. Nevertheless, U.S. couples are clearly more work-intensive than Canadian couples (see Table 7.1).

5.   In the United States in 1992, 25.6 percent of female reference persons under age 65 were married, 27.7 percent had never married, and the remaining 46.8 percent were separated, divorced, or widowed. In contrast, 73.0 percent of male reference persons were married, 15.8 percent had never married, and only 11.3 percent were separated, divorced, or widowed.

6.   The term "single adult" refers to a never-married person aged 18 or over who is not currently living with another adult. He or she may, however, have children living in the household.

7.   In Canada, the median age of nonelderly single adults in 1992 was 33 years, for nonelderly wives it was 39 years, and for nonelderly husbands it was 41 years. Among U.S. residents under age 65, single adults were on average only 28 years old, but the median ages of husbands and wives were the same as in Canada at 41 years and 39 years, respectively.

7

Shallow Income Pools

From the perspective of the political economy of capitalism, poverty is seen largely as a result of the relationship between individuals (who are actual or potential workers) and the labor market. However, there is another perspective to be considered, that of the moral economy of family life (Cheal, 1989). From the latter point of view, the economic well-being of individuals is seen to be shaped by whether or not people occupy a socially defined role within a system of normative obligations to provide mutual support. From a perspective of moral economy, adults who experience poverty are poor either because they do not live with a partner whose income they can share or because their partner is unable, or unwilling,[1] to provide much financial support.

Many of the shallowest income pools are found in the households of unmarried individuals, whose opportunities for sharing are often limited. Consequently, they are overrepresented among the poor. In contrast, married couples who share their incomes are better off than unmarried individuals on average. However, there is considerable diversity of socioeconomic conditions among the married, and some couples are not as well off as others. It is therefore important that the married poor be recognized, and their particular circumstances need to be described.

The poorest couples are often those in which the economic disadvantage of lack of employment by one partner cannot be compensated by income sharing, because the other partner also suffers from a shortage of paid work. Many of the married poor (between two-fifths and two-thirds, depending on the country and how the calculations are made) are in marriages where neither partner is in regular employment (i.e., without full-time work all year). Most of the remaining married poor live in families in which the wage of one member who is in regular employment must be shared with a partner who is not regularly employed. They are especially likely to be poor if the main earner receives only low wages, but it can also happen in large families when the main earner receives a medium wage. The only couples who have no incidence of poverty at all are those in which both husband and wife are employed throughout the year, and both earn medium or high wages. The income pools in these successful dual-career families are clearly superior to all others.

MARRIAGE, WORK, AND MONEY

All husband-wife families potentially have two earners. In practice, not every husband-wife family is a double-income family. The differences between husband-wife families with two earners and other couples deserve to be studied in detail. For example, there is evidence to suggest that, among renters, single-income families have a higher incidence of housing need than do double-income families (Engeland, 1991). Ross, Shillington, and Lochhead (1994) report that in Canada in 1991 it was relatively rare among poor couples for both spouses to be employed as full-time workers for a full year. Not only were these husbands unlikely to be employed as full-year workers, but wives in poor families were much less likely to be fully employed than their counterparts in nonpoor families.

Wives' earnings are increasingly important resources for contemporary families (Vickery, 1979; Foster, 1981; Statistics Canada, 1984b; Shaw, 1986). Women often cite housing costs and other household expenses as the main reasons for working, and their earnings often contribute to making rent and mortgage payments (Brannen & Moss, 1987; 1991). In the United States, wives' earnings contribute between one-fourth and one-third of total husband-wife earnings (Hanson & Ooms, 1991). In the average double-income family in Canada in 1990, the wife's earnings contributed 29.4 percent of the total family income (Statistics Canada, 1992). (The husband's earnings contributed 55.8 percent, with the remainder of family income coming from other family members' earnings, investment income, transfer payments, pensions, and other money income).

Families in which the husband and wife are both employed have higher incomes on average than do one-earner families (McQuillan, 1988; Rashid, 1990b). Wives' earnings play an especially important part in raising the level of household income in families where the husbands' earnings are relatively low. Hanson and Ooms (1991) demonstrated from U.S. Consumer Expenditure Survey data for 1980–83 that the income advantages of dual-earner couples are greatest among low-income families.

Studies of housing affordability invariably identify size of household income as a major determinant of housing consumption (Bird, 1990). Since wives' earnings make an important contribution to the household income in two-earner families, we would expect them to have an impact on house purchase (Myers, 1985).[2] In Canada, Doyle (1985) claims that home ownership is becoming largely the domain of households with two incomes. She thinks that this trend has had an inflationary effect on the housing market, as it is possible for families with two incomes to carry large mortgages in order to finance the purchase of higher-priced houses. Furthermore, she is concerned that this may have contributed to the disadvantaged position of families that depend on only one income, since they must now compete in a housing market that is dominated by double-income families. Similarly, Hall (1993) has argued that in European cities double-income households exert an upward pressure on housing prices, forcing larger and/or less affluent households to seek affordable housing at the urban fringe. Watson (1986) has claimed that in many parts of Britain and Australia couples earning two incomes are frequently the only households for whom home ownership is a viable alternative, since house prices are so high as to be prohibitive for the majority of one-earner households. Consistent with this body of research, U.S. Consumer Expenditure Survey data for 1980–83 show that among husband-wife families with at least one child under age 18, dual earners have an advantage over single earners in their ability to buy a home (Hanson & Ooms, 1991). Dual-earner families are more likely to be home owners than are single-earner families, especially in lower income groups.

Most of the research literature on family work systems in the last two decades has focused on the advantages possessed by two-earner families. For example, Rubin and Riney (1994) have shown that during the period when real wage levels were stagnant in the United States in the 1970s and 1980s, two-earner families in which the wife worked full-time were the only ones to have increased income. However, it is also increasingly recognized today that more attention needs to be paid to the opposite side of the coin. If families with two full-year workers are relatively advantaged, then presumably other families must be relatively disadvantaged (McQuillan, 1988; 1991; Crompton, 1995).

COUPLES' LIFE CHANCES

Work patterns in husband-wife families can be compared in a systematic way, by arraying six types of families ranging from those that are the least involved in the labor market to those that are the most involved. At one extreme, there are the *nonworking* couples in which both partners are completely outside of the labor market. More involved in the labor market, but marginal to it, are couples where the only employment is on a part-year basis *(one partially employed* or *both partially employed)*. The remaining three family types consist of work systems in which at least one member is employed full-year. His or her partner may be not employed, or employed part-year, or employed full-year. Couples in which one partner is regularly employed but the other partner is not employed are *breadwinner-homemaker* families. If one partner is employed full-year, and the second partner is employed part-year, then the family is a *provider-coprovider* family. If both partners are employed full-year then they constitute a *dual-career* family.

Working arrangements in families are typically gendered. That is especially so among older couples influenced by traditional norms and among couples with young children. Women's employment histories are often not as continuous as those of men, since many women withdraw from the labor force temporarily for family-related events (Robinson, 1987). Furthermore, many women choose to work part-time, because of family responsibilities or in order to spend more time at home. In Canada in 1988, 25 percent of employed women were working part-time, compared to just 8 percent of men (Parliament, 1989). For these reasons, the social distribution of family types varies by gender.

Breadwinner-homemaker families and provider-coprovider families are more likely to have men rather than women as the chief wage-earners (see Table 7.1). There is reason to believe that the gender of the chief wage-earner makes a difference to the financial well-being of families. Provider-coprovider families in which the wife is the provider will therefore be analyzed separately from families in which the husband is the provider. Breadwinner-homemaker families in which the wife is the breadwinner will have to be dropped from any further analysis, because there are insufficient cases to produce reliable results for this group.

TABLE 7.1

Relative Frequencies of Family Work Systems among Married Couples with Reference Person Under Age 65, in Canada and the United States (in percent)

Family Work Systems	Canada	United States
Nonworking	7.1	4.7
One Partially Employed	9.1	7.6
Both Partially Employed	10.7	6.4
Husband Breadwinner, Wife Homemaker	14.4	19.4
Wife Breadwinner, Husband Homemaker	2.2	2.0
Husband Provider, Wife Coprovider	24.7	24.2
Wife Provider, Husband Coprovider	7.4	5.4
Dual Career	24.4	30.3

Families in which the husband is the sole breadwinner or the main provider have slightly more children on average than other families. Half or more of them contain children who are less than 13 years of age (see Tables 7.2 and 7.3). In these families, reduced participation in the labor market is largely due to a division of labor between husband and wife, in which the wife is the person most responsible for caring for children. A sharp division of labor is facilitated by the fact that many of these husbands are relatively well educated and therefore have good prospects for individual occupational success and high earnings.

Nonworking couples, on the other hand, present a quite different social profile. They infrequently have co-resident children under age 13, especially in Canada, which is explained by their being much older on average than other couples. The median age of husbands in these families in both Canada and the United States is 59 years, and their wives are typically in the mid-fifties. An extremely low level of participation in the labor market by these families is due mainly to early exit from the labor force with advancing age, either voluntary or (more likely) involuntary. Levels of education are very low for both husbands and wives in these families, which suggests that once they lose a job they are unlikely to get a new one. In the United States, 41.2 percent of husbands in this group of those under age 65 had already retired.[3]

In contrast, couples in which one or both partners are employed only part-year do not have the option of withdrawing from work into retirement, since they are much younger on average. This is an amorphous

TABLE 7.2
Social Characteristics of Types of Married Couples with Reference Person Under Age 65, in Canada

Social Characteristics	Nonworking	One Partially Employed	Both Partially Employed	Husband Breadwinner, Wife Homemaker	Husband Provider, Wife Coprovider	Wife Provider, Husband Coprovider	Dual-career
Age (Median)							
Husband	59.0	45.0	38.0	44.0	39.0	38.0	41.0
Wife	56.0	42.0	35.0	42.0	37.0	35.0	39.0
Post-High School Education (Percent)							
Neither	70.7	60.1	46.9	45.4	33.6	36.7	31.9
One	17.6	23.5	27.0	25.4	24.2	34.0	25.8
Both	11.7	16.4	26.1	29.2	42.2	29.3	42.3
Number of Children (Mean)	0.5	1.0	1.0	1.2	1.3	0.8	0.9
One or More Children Age 0–12 (Percent)	18.1	43.2	48.2	49.6	56.5	40.4	39.2

TABLE 7.3
Social Characteristics of Types of Married Couples with Reference Person Under Age 65, in the United States

Social Characteristics	Nonworking	One Partially Employed	Both Partially Employed	Husband Breadwinner, Wife Homemaker	Husband Provider, Wife Coprovider	Wife Provider, Husband Coprovider	Dual-career
Age (Median)							
Husband	59.0	44.0	39.0	41.0	40.0	43.0	42.0
Wife	54.0	41.0	38.0	38.0	38.0	40.0	39.0
Post-High School Education (Percent)							
Neither	62.8	51.5	41.2	42.3	30.3	51.1	30.8
One	(21.9)	24.2	(19.1)	25.1	24.5	(23.4)	27.6
Both	(15.3)	24.3	39.7	32.6	45.2	25.5	41.6
Number of Children (Mean)	1.0	1.3	1.2	1.4	1.3	0.7	0.9
One or More Children Age 0–12 (Percent)	33.8	49.6	46.1	59.4	57.3	33.2	41.0
Reference Person Retired (Percent)	38.5	(6.4)	0	(0.2)	0	0	0

( ) Indicates cell is <30 cases.

group of people who appear to be struggling to get by. Their education levels are fairly low, especially in Canada, and their job prospects are probably not very good. Many of these couples have children to support, and they therefore need to take whatever work they can find.

Couples in which the wife is the main provider also seem to have had some difficulty in obtaining secure employment, but mainly for the husband. Wives in these couples are more likely than their husbands to have a college or university education. Since these families are small, children are less of a barrier to full-time employment here.

Finally, most dual-career families are well positioned to take advantage of whatever opportunities are provided by the labor market. Educational levels achieved by these couples are high, and they have few children to distract them from occupational pursuits. Furthermore, these families with children are much more likely to have older children (ages 13–17) than they are to have very young children (3 years of age or under). This suggests that in some of these families a dual-career lifestyle was adopted only after the children had reached an age at which they were judged to require less close attention. With all of these advantages, dual-career couples should be the least likely to have serious difficulties in maintaining a satisfactory standard of living — and indeed they are. Dual-career couples have the highest combined incomes, they spend the lowest proportion of their income on necessities, and they have the highest rate of home ownership of all husband-wife families (see tables 7.4 and 7.5).

Today, dual-career families set the standards of consumption to which other families aspire. By comparison with their quality of life, people in other types of families may see themselves as relatively deprived. During a period when many families were able to increase their household incomes by adding a second paycheck, expectations for consumption have risen against a general background of economic stagnation. In this context, families who do not have two full-year earners are likely to find themselves falling behind (Bergmann, 1986), and they have an increased risk of falling into poverty (Ross, Shillington, & Lochhead, 1994).

MARGINALIZATION OF LESS WORK-INTENSIVE FAMILIES

In recent decades, the North American societies have undergone a broad process of intensification of work among nonelderly persons,[4] with some fluctuations according to the economic cycle. The labor force

TABLE 7.4
Economic Characteristics of Types of Married Couples with Reference Person Under Age 65, in Canada

Economic Characteristics	Nonworking	One Partially Employed	Both Partially Employed	Husband Breadwinner, Wife Homemaker	Husband Provider, Wife Coprovider	Wife Provider, Husband Coprovider	Dual-career
Combined Income Before Taxes (Median $)	20,131.00	30,164.00	39,389.00	45,837.00	55,480.00	51,696.00	69,999.00
Combined Income After Taxes (Median $)	19,380.00	26,823.00	32,851.00	35,660.00	43,492.00	41,266.00	53,928.00
Necessities Expenses (Median $)[a]	4,523.00	4,393.75	4,976.67	4,846.00	5,434.25	5,948.25	6,605.50
Necessities Proportion (Median %)[b]	52.8	48.5	45.2	44.6	41.9	41.0	39.9
Home Ownership (%)	69.6	69.2	64.2	80.5	78.0	69.3	81.3

[a]Necessities Expenses = sum of expenditures on food, dwelling and clothes per capita.
[b]Necessities Proportion = Household expenditure on necessities as a proportion of total receipts after all deductions.

TABLE 7.5
Economic Characteristics of Types of Married Couples with Reference Person Under Age 65, in the United States

Economic Characteristics	Nonworking	One Partially Employed	Both Partially Employed	Husband Breadwinner, Wife Homemaker	Husband Provider, Wife Coprovider	Wife Provider, Husband Coprovider	Dual-career
Combined Income Before Taxes (Median $)	4,124.00	14,400.00	27,180.00	31,040.00	42,000.00	33,454.00	51,500.00
Combined Income After Taxes (Median $)	4,124.00	13,200.00	24,368.00	28,506.00	38,000.00	30,000.00	46,124.00
Necessities Expenses (Median $)[a]	3,135.00	3,294.00	3,933.33	4,009.00	4,475.00	4,955.00	5,146.00
Necessities Proportion (Median %)[b]	69.5	52.0	46.0	48.3	39.6	42.8	36.1
Home Ownership (%)	60.6	67.4	65.2	70.9	77.7	74.3	83.8

[a]Necessities Expenses = sum of expenditures on food, dwelling, and clothes per capita.
[b]Necessities Proportion = Consumer Unit expenditure on necessities as a proportion of total receipts after all deductions.

participation rate of youths and young adults rose and, although the participation rate of men over age 55 fell, that was more than offset by the increased participation of women of all ages. As a result, total labor force participation rates in the United States and Canada went up respectively from 69.2 and 63.9 in 1968 to 77.7 and 76.9 in 1988 (Bosch, Dawkins, & Michon, 1993). Employment among young people fell sharply after 1989, but the average total amount of time spent in employment over the life course (i.e., "lifelong working hours") remains high in North America. Sam Rosenberg summarized the pattern of working time in the United States in the early 1990s as follows: "For the individual, some trends point to a reduction in working time and others to an increase in working time. For the family, the picture seems clearer. As the average number of paid workers per family has increased, the average family is working longer hours to maintain its standard of living. Even so, those workers not satisfied with their work schedules are more likely to need more hours and more money. Very few would trade income for leisure time" (1993, p. 289).

In a regime of work intensification, the less work-intensive families are increasingly marginalized. Unmarried mothers who choose to stay at home to raise their children are the classic example of such marginalization. These women have come under great political and administrative pressure in North America as expectations about the employment of mothers have grown. Married-couple families who are not heavily involved in the labor market also run the risk of being marginalized. Here it is the unseen hand of the market, rather than the pressure of public opinion, that tends to relegate these families to the margins. Couples in which the wife or husband, or both partners, reduce paid working time in order to be with their children may lack the earning power to compete with more work-intensive families for housing and consumer goods.

The 1992 U.S. and Canadian consumer expenditure surveys both show that, when husband-wife families under age 65 have neither partner employed full-year, then they are usually not well off (see Tables 7.4 and 7.5). These couples have low incomes,[5] they spend large proportions of their incomes on necessities, and their rates of home ownership are lower than in other families.[6] Couples in which neither partner is employed full-year are overrepresented in the poorest quintile of income and expenditure, although the extent of overrepresentation depends on whether calculations are made per capita or per reference equivalent (see Tables 7.6 and 7.7). These families may require public financial support.

TABLE 7.6

Percentage of Households with Reference Person Under Age 65 in Poverty Quintiles by Family Types, in Canada

Poverty Quintiles	Nonworking	One Partially Employed	Both Partially Employed	Husband Breadwinner, Wife Homemaker	Husband Provider, Wife Coprovider	Wife Provider, Husband Coprovider	Dual-career
Lowest Quintile							
Income Per Capita	51.4	44.1	24.4	19.3	10.3	8.1	3.9
Income Per Reference	47.8	29.0	13.3	6.3	3.1	(1.6)	(1.9)
Total Receipts Per Capita	48.0	44.6	27.2	28.6	15.5	10.7	6.2
Total Receipts Per Reference	44.6	28.4	14.4	11.4	4.5	(2.6)	2.7
Necessities Expenses	39.7	41.6	27.9	30.8	22.2	18.3	12.7
Highest Quintile							
Necessities Proportion	34.6	24.4	14.5	13.5	10.0	(7.1)	6.2

() Indicates cell is <30 cases.

TABLE 7.7

Percentage of Consumer Units with Reference Person Under Age 65 in Poverty Quintiles by Family Types, in the United States

Poverty Quintiles	Nonworking	One Partially Employed	Both Partially Employed	Husband Breadwinner, Wife Homemaker	Husband Provider, Wife Coprovider	Wife Provider, Husband Coprovider	Dual-career
Lowest Quintile							
Income Per Capita	58.8	45.2	22.7	20.0	10.9	(8.7)	(3.2)
Income Per Reference	53.5	32.7	(8.3)	12.1	(5.6)	(3.6)	(1.6)
Total Receipts Per Capita	53.9	45.9	23.2	25.8	13.0	(8.3)	5.4
Total Receipts Per Reference	50.8	34.3	(9.8)	16.5	6.5	(3.9)	(2.1)
Necessities Expenses	43.3	40.6	30.0	24.3	20.3	(19.7)	13.4
Highest Quintile							
Necessities Proportion	44.0	28.4	(17.8)	19.0	9.4	(10.3)	6.0

( ) Indicates cell is <30 cases.

SUPPORT FOR FAMILIES WITHOUT WORK

In the United States, 20–30 percent of the husband-wife families in which neither partner was employed full-year in 1992 had received welfare payments or unemployment compensation payments. In Canada, between 45 percent and 75 percent of such families received financial support in one form or the other. Interestingly, nonworking couples under age 65 fall at the bottom end of the range of public financial support in both countries. This suggests that in the North American income-support systems there are strong disincentives for entire families to give up all work.

Nonworking couples are the most likely of husband-wife families to use welfare programs (34.7 percent of them in Canada and 18.9 percent of them in the United States in 1992). In contrast, working families in which there is some employment interruption are more likely to be users of unemployment insurance (UI). In the United States, receipt of UI occurred most often among couples in which just one partner was partially employed in 1992 (20.0 percent), or where both partners were partially employed (27.3 percent), or in which the wife was the provider and the husband was a coprovider (25.8 percent). In Canada, 57.3 percent of couples with just one person employed for a part of 1992 received UI payments, and 69.9 percent of couples with both partners partially employed received such payments. When the wife was the main income provider and the husband was a coprovider, 60.7 percent of couples received UI payments at some time during the year. Also, couples where the husband was the provider and the wife was a coprovider had received UI benefits in 37.6 percent of cases in Canada (cf. 7.7 percent in the United States).

Clearly, formal financial support systems can be important means by which married couples manage the changing relationship between themselves and the labor market. That was especially true of Canadian families in the early 1990s.

CHILDREN, FAMILY WORK
SYSTEMS AND SUPPORT SYSTEMS

Welfare payments and unemployment compensation payments are made to adults, but children are often major beneficiaries of these transfers. That is because the economic fortunes of children are inextricably linked to the employment statuses of their parents (Lichter & Eggebeen, 1994). When their parents are out of work, or working part-time, the well-being of children depends on how parents mobilize alternative resources. Indirectly, children's lives may come to depend upon financial supports that their parents receive from public agencies.

In North America, and especially in Canada, large numbers of children potentially benefit from welfare programs and UI programs. In the United States, these two types of programs combined help support 62.1 percent of the children of nonworking couples, 32.9 percent of children in two-parent families where just one parent is employed part-year, 37.0 percent of children both of whose parents are only partially employed, and 31.6 percent of the children of a mother who is the main income provider and a father who is a coprovider. In Canada, UI and welfare programs help to support more than three-fourths of children in families where neither parent is employed full-year. Specifically, benefits are received by the households of 80.1 percent of the children of nonworking couples, 77.6 percent of the children of couples in which only one partner is partially employed, 82.1 percent of the children of couples where both partners are partially employed, 68.2 percent of the children of couples where the wife is the income provider and the husband is a coprovider, and 38.9 percent of the children of couples where the husband is the income provider and the wife is a coprovider.

Children's economic experiences that are due to parents' participation in the labor market are clearly often mediated by public transfers, especially in Canada. Children are often the invisible beneficiaries of income-support programs for adults, and the effect of programs such as UI on children's lives needs to be made more visible. The accessibility of income-support programs, and the level and duration of the support that they provide, are important considerations for children's lives in post-modern societies. Cuts that were made to these programs after 1992 cannot have left children unharmed.

DISCUSSION

In this chapter we have examined the fact that, while marriage provides a barrier against poverty for many people, it also increases the risk of poverty for some people. At one extreme, married persons who are employed full-year at medium or high wages and whose spouses are also employed full-year at medium or high wages have no risk of poverty to speak of. At the other extreme are the married poor where neither partner is in regular employment. We have seen that the social formation of poverty in families is structured by the linked lives of husbands and wives and of parents and children. This fact is well known at a common-sense level, but it has not been so easy to express in social theory. In the dominant theories of economic inequality, the emphasis has tended to be placed on studying the political economy of markets, corporations, and states. There is a clear need for a recasting of the sociology of stratification that takes account of family structures and the ways in which they are changing.

Until very recently, the principal accounts of inequality by sociologists consisted of analyzing differential occupational attainments, or "class" positions, of male family heads (Crompton & Mann, 1986). Underlying this approach was an implicit assumption about the universality in industrial societies of breadwinner-homemaker families, composed of a husband who works full-time all year to earn the family income and a wife who looks after the needs of her husband and children. According to the "family wage" theory of stratification, it is the husband's occupational role that determines the socioeconomic position of the family as a unit. Inequality is seen as the result of the capitalist market for labor, in which workers with different levels of skill earn different incomes. The family's economic position, and its level of well-being, are described as the result of the earning power of the husband, who is therefore labelled the head of the family.

In recent decades, a series of changes have occurred that make traditional models of occupational attainment less useful for explaining inequalities between families than they were in the past. The greater complexity of economic inequality today, as well as increased awareness of the social distribution of paid and unpaid labor, have helped provoke a crisis in sociological theories of stratification (Mann, 1986). Perhaps the most obvious empirical change is the substantial increase in the number of female-headed sole-parent families, whose situation was described in an earlier chapter. Clearly, theories that were based on models of men's work histories will not always be relevant to those families that are headed by women.

More relevant to the themes of the present chapter is the fact that there has been a substantial increase in the number of double-income families. In many cases it is no longer the male breadwinner's family wage that supports the family; rather, it is a combination of the earnings of husband and wife. Related to this, there has been an increase in part-time workers, many of whom are married women. These changes mean that inequalities between families are no longer determined mainly by the inequalities in wages between full-year (male) workers. We saw one of the results of that shift in the previous chapter, in the lesser significance of low wages by comparison with the distribution of work as the principal cause of poverty at the end of the twentieth century. In this chapter we have seen another result, namely, the impact of the intensity of family participation in the labor market upon the social distribution of poverty. In the next chapter, we shall see how work and income are distributed over the life course and the effect that has on the chances of avoiding poverty at different ages.

NOTES

1. In some marriages, personal incomes may not be fully shared. The possibility therefore exists that one partner can be poor while the other partner is comparatively well off. Since husbands' wages are generally higher than wives' wages, it is most likely that married women would be more adversely affected by this than married men. Unfortunately, neither the Canadian Family Expenditure Survey nor the U.S. Consumer Expenditure Survey contains information on income-sharing practices. It is therefore not feasible to calculate the prevalence of intrafamilial poverty here. The married poverty described in this report should therefore be considered as a minimum estimate. For a relevant discussion see Graham (1987).

2. It seems that wives' earnings had only a small effect on families' housing before the mid-1970s. Using 1971 Canadian census data, Marion Steele (1979) concluded that the addition of a second earner (who was assumed to be the wife) in fact made little difference to house purchasing decisions. She argued that this was the case in part because institutional lenders at the time generally ignored wives' earnings in calculating a household's ability to service mortgage debt. She also thought that many families did not include wives' incomes as a factor in their housing decisions, because women's earnings were seen as transient and of lesser importance.

Conditions today are not the same as they were in the 1970s. The degree and type of involvement in the labor force by married women has changed and, as more wives have become employed at better jobs, the policies of institutional lenders have also changed. Husbands' attitudes toward wives' earnings may have altered too, although it is hard to be sure. Danes and Winter (1990) report that in the United States, differences in home ownership rates between one-earner and two-earner households can be observed now that were not apparent in the data before 1977. They believe that this is because in the earlier period wives' incomes were discounted, either by lenders or by the families themselves, but this is no longer the case.

3. Statistics on the retired are not available from the 1992 Canadian Family Expenditure Survey public use file, in which the retired are unfortunately included with the unemployed as "not working."

4.   As work has intensified in the population considered to be of "working age," so the extent of full-time work over the life course has shrunk, and the period in which someone is considered to be of normal working age has narrowed. In particular, the socially defined timing of the onset of becoming "elderly" has fallen. For some purposes now, being a senior citizen is considered to start at age 55. In the present study old age is conventionally defined as beginning at 65, which is still the "normal" age of retirement according to many pension plans in North America. However, as Table 7.3 shows, that is an increasingly problematic benchmark. The average age of retirement for men in Canada today is around 60.

5.   Income data on individuals in the U.S. Consumer Expenditure Survey are not reported here for those cases designated by the Bureau of Labor Statistics as "incomplete income reporters," in order to avoid presenting income figures that are artificially low.

6.   Home ownership rates are generally only weakly related to current employment status. Over half of husband-wife families below age 65 in which neither partner is presently a full-year employee nevertheless own their own homes. Even among nonworking couples, 60 percent (United States) or more (Canada) are homeowners. Many couples who are now either unemployed or underemployed became so only after a period of intensive work for pay, during which they were able to purchase homes. Variations in home ownership rates are therefore not large between different types of families in the over-35 age groups. In contrast, the negative impact of lack of employment on owning property is very strong in husband-wife families where the reference person is 35 years of age or under. Approximately two-thirds of young dual-career couples own their own homes. However, less than half of young underemployed couples do so, and less than one-fourth of young couples who are unemployed are homeowners.

8

The Economic Life Course

The capacity of a male breadwinner to earn a family wage sufficient to meet his own needs and those of his wife and children has been the classical basis for estimating the incidence of poverty.[1] Applied to the life course, this approach inspired the idea that there is a cycle of rising and falling risk of poverty as demands on the family income wax and wane with family growth and, later, contraction in family size. This model of the economic life course was initiated by Rowntree at the end of the nineteenth century. It was revived by family life cycle theorists in the middle of the twentieth century, and it was subsequently refined in life cycle models of family welfare (Axinn & Levin, 1979). According to family life cycle theory, the challenges of avoiding poverty due to family formation and retirement from paid work are critical transition points in the normal life cycle.

Rowntree's study of the working classes of provincial England led him to conclude that the life of a wage laborer was marked by three periods of economic stress (see Figure 8.1). The first of these periods of poverty began at, or soon after, birth. Throughout most of childhood the probability of being poor was high, due to the inadequacy of the average man's wage to support a number of dependents. When children grew older and they began to earn wages, from age 14 onward, they helped to lift the family out of poverty. During the stage of youth and early adulthood wages exceeded the demands of family responsibilities, and so this was a

FIGURE 8.1

Avoiding Income Poverty Over the Life Course, York, 1899

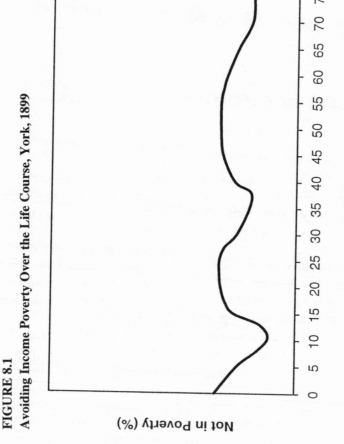

Source: B. Seebohm Rowntree. *Poverty* (London: Macmillan, 1902).

period of comparative prosperity. At least, it could be a period of prosperity, if the adult children remained at home and shared expenses with their parents.

With marriage, at about age 25, a new phase of family formation began that would lead to another cycle of poverty due to the stress of supporting young children. From age 30 through age 40, as children were born and family size increased, poverty deepened. Eventually, the parents could expect to enjoy a new period of prosperity, when their children began to earn wages. However, if there were more than three children in the family, relief from poverty was likely to be delayed.

Throughout middle age, from approximately age 40 through age 64, the family breadwinner and his wife were not likely to suffer from serious economic stress. This long phase with no children under working age to support must have been the least stressful part of the life course. Nevertheless, the average laborer's wage was not sufficient to permit him to save enough for himself and his wife to live on, should they ever be without an income. Inevitably, then, in old age, when the laborer was no longer fit for regular work, he and his wife fell back into poverty. Their meager savings were quickly exhausted and this final period of poverty was usually very difficult, especially when the man died and his widow was left alone.

Rowntree's conclusions about poverty and the life cycle at the end of the nineteenth century had a considerable influence on social policy in the twentieth century, especially concerning income transfers to families with children and the elderly. How has the relevance of Rowntree's model been affected by the introduction of those programs, and by other changes during the past hundred years?

In 1936, Rowntree himself repeated his famous study of poverty conducted in York in 1899, in order to determine what changes had occurred in the living conditions of workers over the intervening 37 years (Rowntree, 1941). Despite the general economic progress that he recorded, the life cycle pattern of poverty in the working-class population had not changed very much. The people least affected by poverty were still the young adults, aged 15–24 (23.7 percent poor), and those in middle age, 45–64 (20.7 percent poor). Adults in the prime childbearing ages, 25–44, were more likely to be poor (28.8 percent), but the worst off were the elderly, aged 65 and over (47.5 percent), and especially the children (under age 1, 52.5 percent were poor, and from ages 1 through 4, 49.7 percent were poor).

Two differences should be noted between Rowntree's data on poverty in 1936 and his impression of the age distribution of poverty in 1899. First, adults in the childbearing years, aged 25–44, do not seem to have been as poor in 1936 as they were 37 years earlier. This decline may have been due to a fall in average fertility in the intervening period. Second, Rowntree's 1936 analysis showed that the risk of poverty was highest among very young children, whereas in 1899 he thought that children under five years of age were relatively well off. Rowntree appears to have thought that greater poverty among older children in the earlier period was due to the birth of additional children into the family as the child aged. However, it is not clear what explanation, if any, he had for the very high rate of poverty among the youngest children in the mid-1930s.

After the 1930s, fertility rose in the post–World War II period before falling again. Today, the average risk of poverty in the 25–44 age group is not likely to be very high. One important change has been a steady increase in employment among wives. For mothers with newborn children who are unable to gain access to high-quality daycare, the impact of employment interruption on the risk of poverty in the first year of life must be greater now than it was in Rowntree's time.

Changes in fertility and in mothers' employment are two important factors to keep in mind when comparing the end of the nineteenth century with the end of the twentieth century. However, these changes are eclipsed by the changes that occurred at the other end of the life course. In all of the Anglo-American countries, the dominant theme in the story about changing financial well-being and the life course has been the growing economic security of the elderly (Hedström & Ringen, 1987).

The principal reason for improvement in the economic conditions of the elderly has been the maturation of government pension schemes. The proportion of the population covered by these schemes, and the benefit levels paid, increased through the early 1990s. In the post–World War II period, the incomes of people aged 65 and over improved significantly relative to the general population (Lindsay & Donald, 1988). Although the average income of elderly people continues to be lower than the national average in Canada and the United States, their poverty rate has fallen to a point at which most of the elderly no longer have an unusually high risk of being poor (Gauthier, 1991; Ross, Shillington, & Lochhead, 1994). Unlike other age groups, almost all of the elderly are covered by income support schemes that are designed to keep them out of poverty. It is important to know how far that development has affected the life course distribution of economic security, compared with a century ago.

POVERTY AND AGE IN NORTH AMERICA

Examining the life course distribution of poverty means changing the unit of analysis from the household, or consumer unit, which has been the basis for most of the present study, to the individual as the unit of analysis. The 1992 Consumer Expenditure Survey of the United States and the 1992 Family Expenditure Survey of Canada permit this change in the unit of analysis, though with different degrees of difficulty. Output from the U.S. Consumer Expenditure Survey includes both a file of consumer units and a file of the individual members of the consumer units. Using the members' file, the economic life course can be easily constructed by plotting individual or household economic characteristics against members' ages. Life course analysis using Canadian Family Expenditure Survey data, on the other hand, is more complex.

In the Family Expenditure Survey, full individual-level data are provided only for the reference person and his or her spouse. Individual-level data are not available for children aged 0–17 or for unmarried adult household members other than the reference person. The most serious difficulty here concerns the treatment of adults aged 18–24. In Canada, the majority of young adults are neither household reference persons nor spouses of reference persons, since they tend to live at home with their parents or in other shared accommodations. These youths are typically one of the least visible sections of the population.

In order to overcome the limitations of the Family Expenditure Survey for life course analysis, the household reference person was taken as the unit of analysis for adults age 25 and over, and synthetic data sets were constructed for children aged 0–17 and for youths aged 18–24. Life course data with the individual as the unit of analysis were produced from the public use file for the Family Expenditure Survey in three stages. First, a file of children was created by reproducing household records by the number of times that there were children of a given age category in the household. (The children's age categories were 0–3, 4–6, 7–9, 10–12, 13–15, and 16–17.) None of these children were household reference persons. Apart from individual age categorization, all available data for children are therefore at the household level (which includes the characteristics of the reference person for the child's household). Second, a file of youths was created by reproducing household records by the number of times that there were adults aged 18–24 in the household. In a minority of cases these young adults were household reference persons, for whom a range of data were available. However, in the majority of cases the only individual-level data was age group membership. Third, in households with a reference person age 25 or over the reference person was taken to be the unit of analysis. Full individual-level data as well as household-level data were available for this sample of adults. However, it should be recognized that this is only a partial sample of the population over age 24, because it does not include spouses of reference persons or other co-resident adults age 25 or older.

The validity of this procedure for studying the social distribution of poverty was tested by applying it to the file of consumer units taken from the U.S. Consumer Expenditure Survey and comparing the results against data from the Consumer Expenditure Survey members' file. The age distributions of poverty for the members' file and for synthetic files of children and youths were identical. There were some minor discrepancies between data from the members' file and the sample of reference persons age 25 and over, due to the differing economic characteristics of women who are reference persons compared with other women. Female reference persons, who are often sole parents, have smaller available incomes on average than other women, most of whom are involved in some form of income sharing with men. As a result, poverty data for female reference persons are not representative of all women. Data on reference persons therefore tend to overstate the actual rate of poverty by two or three percentage points. With this qualification, the procedure used to construct life course data from the Canadian Family Expenditure Survey was judged to produce a reasonable estimate of the age profile of economic life chances at the population level. However, it is obviously not as accurate as if separate data had been collected for every individual in the original survey, and caution may be needed in the interpretation of data for subpopulations. In this regard, the Consumer Expenditure Survey should be considered the more authoritative information source in the present chapter.

Following the procedures outlined above, it is possible to compare the economic characteristics of different age groups in the U.S. and Canadian populations in 1992. To begin, economic comparisons will be made for income poverty, considered as a relative lack of total money receipts after all deductions. Comparison will be made in two ways, for income per capita and for income per reference equivalent. These two measures have previously been shown to produce different kinds of results. We shall see that this is also true of life course trends in poverty and poverty avoidance. In order to compare the economic fortunes of U.S. and Canadian residents at different ages, the poverty line employed here will be 50 percent of national median income. That is to say, individuals whose total money receipts after all deductions per capita or per reference equivalent are less than half the median income for their country are considered to be poor. A final methodological point is that graphic presentation of the data in a form comparable to Rowntree's chart of the three periods of economic stress necessitates reversing the normal measurement emphasis, from the incidence of poverty to the incidence of poverty avoidance (see Figures 8.2 and 8.3).

ESCAPING FROM POVERTY

For individuals who lack economic security, staying out of poverty, and escaping from poverty once they have fallen into it, are serious pre-occupations. What proportions of the different age groups avoided poverty in Canada and the United States in 1992? How does their experience compare with Rowntree's model of the economic life course in England in earlier times? Figures 8.2 and 8.3 illustrate the relationship between individual age and the probability of not being poor. They show that, in North America in the early 1990s, the chances of avoiding poverty were not distributed over the life course in exactly the same manner that Rowntree described in 1899 or in 1936. The main point of similarity between then and now lies in the prevalence of poverty among children under age 13.

In Canada, preteen children of all ages are more likely to be poor than adults of any age, including the oldest among the elderly,[2] although the differences are small when income is adjusted using the equivalence scale. In the United States, the tendency for children to have the highest rates of poverty is very strong. The differences between the youngest children and adults over age 40 are large when income is calculated per capita. When income is calculated per reference equivalent, the youngest children in the United States still have the highest risk of being poor, but children aged 4–12 are very slightly more likely to avoid poverty than young adults aged 18–24 or people in extreme old age, that is, 86 years and older. Overall, children are among the poorest, if not the very poorest, members of our societies today, as they also were in the 1930s and before that at the end of the nineteenth century.

As U.S. and Canadian children get older, more of them escape from poverty. Based on per capita income, there is a steady improvement in economic security through childhood and youth into full adulthood. When income is measured per reference equivalent, however, the position of U.S. youths in the 18–24 age group deteriorates, although that is not the

FIGURE 8.2
Avoiding Income Poverty Over the Life Course, United States, 1992

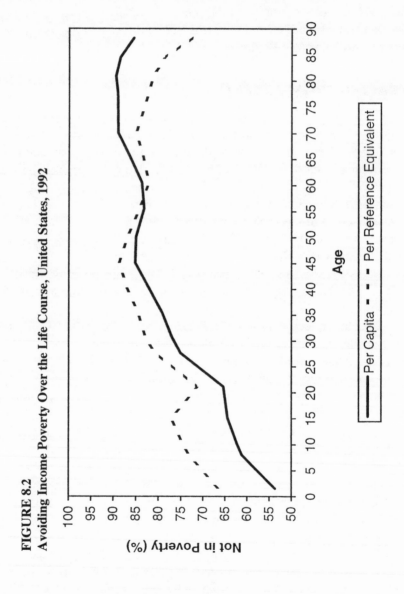

FIGURE 8.3
Avoiding Income Poverty Over the Life Course, Canada, 1992

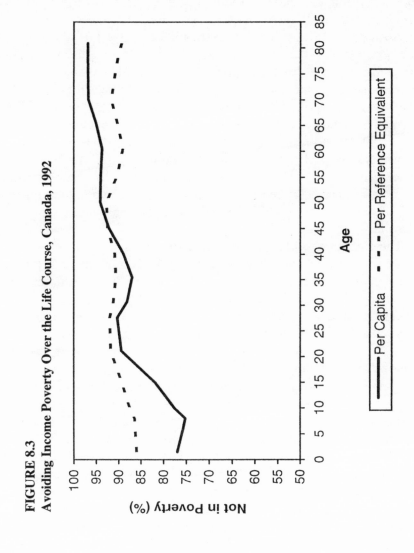

case in Canada. According to Rowntree's model, this stage in the life course should be a period of comparative affluence. The fall in the rate of poverty avoidance among U.S. youths therefore suggests that a new form of poverty may have emerged in postmodern society. Clearly, that is a subject requiring more research, using other data sets that have more information about individual employment histories and living arrangements.

According to Rowntree's model of the economic life course in York, the second period of stress occurs at ages 25–44, due to increased financial pressure for the support of children that is not matched by correspondingly rapid increases in wages. A slight increase in poverty for this age group could still be found in Canada in 1992, especially when income is calculated per capita. However, no such tendency existed in the United States in that year. The number of U.S. residents in poverty falls continuously until age 45 or 50, depending on the manner in which income deficiency is calculated. It appears that the second period of economic stress described by Rowntree is no longer a regular feature of the life course in the United States, and it is only weakly present in Canada.

The final period of economic stress in Rowntree's model of the life course occurs in old age, beginning at age 65. It is at this stage that some of the greatest changes in the incidence of poverty have occurred. Most of the attention here has focused on improvements in the economic position of elderly retirees. Until 1973 the poverty rate for the elderly in the United States was substantially higher than the rate for children; since 1973 it has been lower, and it is now substantially lower (Danziger & Weinberg, 1994). However, this is not the only interesting change. Today, the onset of economic difficulties in the latter part of the life course starts much sooner than age 65. In the United States, the incidence of poverty avoidance rises until approximately age 45 (age 50 in Canada), after which it slides until age 65 when it rises once more, before trending down in late old age. The elderly in the United States today clearly benefit from the widespread availability of pensions. Pension income even appears to lift some people out of the preretirement poverty that is due to the serious fall in average earnings in late middle age (see Figure 8.4).[3]

In Canada, any increase in income poverty among the elderly is small, and it occurs only for net income per reference equivalent. The Canadian elderly are never quite as poor as Canadian children. Elderly people in the United States, on the other hand, experience a steep drop in the probability of avoiding poverty in advanced old age. (Note that data reported here on

FIGURE 8.4
Male Reference Person Income Before Taxes Over the
Adult Life Course, Canada and the United States

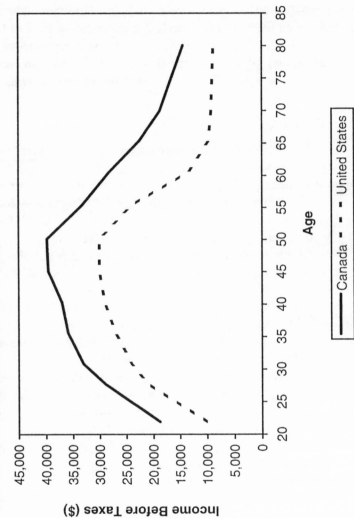

the elderly are not directly comparable for the United States and Canada at the top end, because the highest age category in the Canadian Family Expenditure Survey is 76 years and over, whereas in the U.S. Consumer Expenditure Survey it is 90 years and over.) As already observed, the very oldest U.S. residents (86+) are as likely to be poor as U.S. children when income is adjusted per reference equivalent. However, when income is adjusted per capita the U.S. elderly are consistently better off than children or young adults under age 25. Once having escaped from the poverty of childhood and youth, it seems that most U.S. and Canadian residents are unlikely to be at such high risk of impoverishment ever again.

THE LIFE COURSE GRADIENT

Comparisons between contemporary North America and England at the end of the nineteenth century have a great deal to tell us about the changing requirements for the sociology of poverty. Rowntree's analysis of poverty in 1899 helped to inspire family life cycle theory, with its descriptions of life cycle stages and transition points. In the United States and Canada today, poverty cycles are much less evident than a *poverty gradient*. Children born into poverty gradually climb out of it, and people are generally less likely to be poor in the latter stages of the life course than they are in the early stages. We have already seen part of the explanation for this gradient in the systemic poverty of children. Owing to the neutrality of fiscal policies, and the failures of corporations and governments to meet the needs of families with children, reproduction is a private cost that is paid mainly by the parents.

Faced with persistent child poverty, it may be asked why the mid-life phase of economic stress that Rowntree identified with the childbearing stage of the family life cycle has almost disappeared. Part of the answer to this question is that, as fertility has fallen below the replacement level, there are fewer and fewer large families. Families with several children tend to be poor, but since there are not many of them they have little impact on the poverty rates for different age groups.

A second part of the explanation is that for many wage-earners today the contemporary distribution of incomes over the life course is structured by career paths that bring progressively higher wages with longer work experience, up to about age 50 (see Figure 8.4). The early industrial working class had a narrow range of skills, few promotion prospects and short promotion ladders, as well as few financial incentives for either corporate loyalty or investment in human capital. In contrast, many people in the United States and Canada in the second half of the twentieth century engage in extensive career preparation and career development, from which they gain larger incomes as their skills increase and as they acquire higher positions in organizational hierarchies. In late twentieth-century North America, the period of the life course in which childbearing creates increased demands for consumption coincides with the period in which earnings are also increasing for many people. The result is that the financial pressures created by dependent children, which were frequently overwhelming in the nineteenth century, are often relieved by upward occupational mobility today. However, one implication of this argument is that if economic stagnation in the 1990s causes upward mobility to be severely curtailed, then mid-life poverty can be expected to reappear by the turn of the century.

A third factor that has ameliorated the incidence of poverty among adults with children is the increased tendency for wives to work outside the home and to work for longer hours at better jobs. Except when children are very young, most mothers are now engaged in some paid employment. If the father's wage is low, then the mother's earnings can help to keep the family out of poverty. In working-class couples, where low wages are the result of little education, wives' increased labor compensates for lack of human capital. Wives' employment is associated with a greater probability of home ownership and a lower probability of overcrowding (Cheal, 1993c).

The life course gradient of greater financial security with advancing age is most evident with respect to the accumulation of assets, such as ownership of a home (see Figure 8.5). The rate of home ownership increases rapidly in early adulthood and continues to increase steadily, if less spectacularly, through middle age. In old age there is some evidence of dissaving or, in other words, the liquidation of assets, especially in the lower value of homes owned by the elderly in Canada (not shown here). Nevertheless, impressive numbers of the elderly in Canada and the United States retain the security of owning their own homes. Households and consumer units headed by persons over age 65 not only have lower rates of income poverty than domestic units headed by young adults, but most of the elderly also have greater protection from market fluctuations in rents.

FIGURE 8.5
Home Ownership Over the Adult Life Course, Canada and the United States

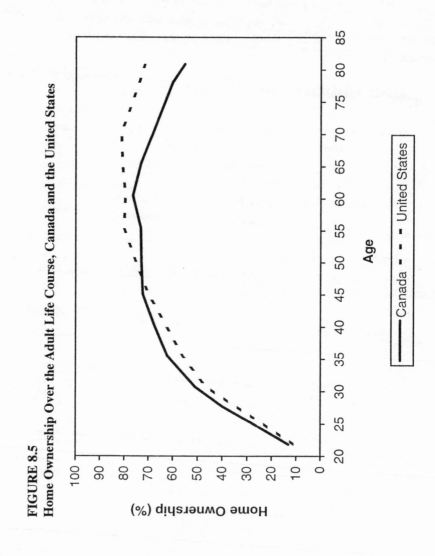

INTERGENERATIONAL CONSUMPTION
CLEAVAGES

Research on old age prior to the 1970s invariably described the elderly as a financially impoverished and socially dependent section of the population (e.g., Townsend, 1957). In some places that image of old people has continued up to the present day, even though conditions have changed in certain significant respects. The financial position of the elderly in general has improved considerably over the past three decades. Some old people are still poor, but poverty today tends to be found in particular subpopulations (such as widows) rather than for the elderly as a whole. There are a number of reasons for the improved financial well-being of the elderly, but two of them are especially important. The expanded coverage and enhanced benefits provided by state income support programs has had the intended effect of lifting many old people out of poverty. Also, many people who are retiring today have benefited from purchasing their homes during the period of social reconstruction after World War II, which was followed by periods of rapid inflation in house prices in subsequent decades. It is mainly the combination of increased transfers from the state and — for the more affluent elderly — the appreciation in the value of their assets that is responsible for the economic security enjoyed by most elderly people today (Danziger & Weinberg, 1994).

In contrast, the working-age population has not fared as well. The standard of living of working people depends on the incomes that they earn, and the real value of their earnings has tended to stagnate and even decline. Over the past two to three decades there has been a tendency for the value of wages to be eroded by price inflation and (in Canada) by higher rates of taxation on earned incomes. Furthermore, in recent years people have felt the effects of the economic restructuring that has produced high rates of unemployment.

These economic facts do not tell the whole story about the changing fortunes of different generations. There are also subjective factors, which influence perceptions of relative well-being and relative deprivation. Katherine Newman (1993) has recently reported some of those subjective influences, in her ethnographic study of a U.S. suburb. Older people and their adult children in the baby-boom generation make intergenerational comparisons in different ways. As a result they tend to arrive at different, and sometimes conflicting, conclusions about recent changes. Today's elderly, many of whom grew up and came to adulthood in difficult times, are generally grateful to have a comfortable standard of living. They tend to be puzzled by, and somewhat suspicious of, complaints made by their children that it is no longer easy to be financially successful. The children born in the post–World War II baby boom grew up with the expectation of a constantly increasing standard of living as a permanent feature of modern life. Many of them are disappointed to find that this is not necessarily the case, and they are afraid that things are only getting worse. For most baby boomers a high standard of living has been a natural assumption, on which all other calculations are based. However, maintaining a high standard of living is proving to be a struggle for many people, and impossible for some of them.

Intergenerational comparisons in North America today are no longer what they were 20 or 30 years ago. The dominant image of the elderly among the nonelderly is changing, from that of a financially impoverished and socially dependent group to that of a financially secure and socially privileged group (Thomson, 1989a). At the same time, intergenerational comparisons are acquiring an emotional charge, which seems likely to make the political economy of aging more volatile than it was in the recent past.

The socioeconomic divisions between individuals and families at different stages of the life course can be illustrated from a random sample survey conducted in the city of Winnipeg, Canada, in 1988. The present author was the principal investigator for the 1988 Winnipeg Area Study, which was carried out under the direction of Raymond F. Currie, University of Manitoba. Interviews were conducted in 528 households, in which detailed questions were asked about the respondents' household arrangements and their financial affairs. The response rate for the eligible households sampled was 72 percent. Comparing the survey data with the 1986 Canadian Census shows that the age distribution of the sample was representative of the adult population in Winnipeg (Currie, 1988). A major goal in research on the 1988 Winnipeg Area Study has been comparative analysis of households of different types. For the purpose of intergenerational comparisons nine household types were identified and their life chances were evaluated. The nine household types are:

sole parent family, with one or more children under age 18;

one person, age 18-44;

married couple, husband's age 18-44, with one or more children under age 5 (additional children age 5 or over may also be present in the household);

married couple, husband's age 18-44, with one or more children all aged 5-17;

married couple, husband's age 18-44, no children;

one person, age 45-64;

married couple, husband's age 45-64, with one or more children under age 18;

married couple, husband's age 45-64, no children;

elderly, age 65 or over (one person or married couple).

The life chances of people in Winnipeg were assessed, first, through a group of questions on the degree of subjective satisfaction with the material conditions of existence. Respondents were asked to rank themselves on a scale of one to seven according to the level of their satisfaction or dissatisfaction with the following four items: their house or apartment as a place to live; the amount of money they have for clothes and other personal expenses; the amount of money they have to spend on things for the home; and the amount of money they have to spend on the people they love. The mean scores on these life chance satisfaction items are presented for each household type in Table 8.1.

TABLE 8.1
Mean Satisfaction with Material Conditions, Winnipeg, 1988

Household Type	Housing	Clothes	Home	Loved Ones
Sole-parent Family[a]	(4.6)	(3.2)	(3.2)	(3.1)
One Person, Age <45	4.8	3.6	3.6	3.8
Married Couple, Husband's Age <45, Child <5	5.2	3.9	3.9	3.9
Married Couple, Husband's Age <45, Child 5-17	5.2	4.6	4.3	4.6
Married Couple, Husband's Age <45, No Children	5.5	4.3	4.4	4.3
One Person, Age 45-64	5.4	4.4	4.5	5.1
Married Couple, Husband's Age 45-64, Child <18	5.4	4.7	4.6	4.4
Married Couple, Husband's Age 45-64, No Children	6.3	5.3	5.6	5.1
Elderly, Age 65+[b]	6.3	5.7	5.5	5.3

[a]Includes one adult and her/his children under age 18.
[b]Includes one person age 65+ or married couple, husband's age 65+.
( ) Indicates cell is <30 cases.

In Winnipeg, respondents in households headed by an elderly person and married couples aged 45–64 with no co-resident children are the most satisfied with their material conditions. Conversely, sole-parent family heads and individuals under age 45 living on their own are the least satisfied. Married couples with children fall between these two extremes, having low to moderate levels of satisfaction. The younger the children, and the younger the parents, the less satisfied these couples are likely to be.

Further information about the life chances of different generations was obtained from twelve questions in the Winnipeg Area Study, dealing with possible strategies that people may adopt to cope with a period of financial difficulty. In principle, there are two main ways of coping with a shortage of money for daily living. One way is to economize by spending less on a number of customary purchases. The other solution is to increase the size of disposable income, either by lowering the cost of housing (which is the largest single item in most household budgets) or by finding an additional source of income.

The questions in the 1988 Winnipeg Area Study on what people do when they face hard times asked respondents if they and their family had been forced to cut expenditures during the last three years on the following items of consumption: home improvements and renovations; furniture; vacations; eating out and other forms of entertainment; medical, dental, and optometrists' services; food; heat and lighting; and clothing. They were then asked if they or other members of their household had done any of the following things during the past three years: moved into cheaper accommodations in order to save money; taken on an extra job in order to add to the household income; received welfare assistance; or received financial help from relatives.

With the sole exception of health expenditures, the elderly are consistently the least likely to report having cut back on their spending during the last three years. On the other hand, families with children, especially young children, are the most likely to have made such cuts. Married couples with children under age 5 in which the husband is under age 45 are seven and one-half times more likely than the elderly to have cut back on vacations, nearly five times more likely to have cut back on furniture purchases, four times more likely to have cut spending on clothes, and three times more likely to have cut back on eating out and entertainment as well as home improvements and renovations. Especially troubling is the fact that they are nearly six times more likely to have cut back on food and seven times more likely to have cut back on heat and lighting.[4]

Not surprisingly, young families in Winnipeg are much more likely than the elderly to be forced to take difficult or unpleasant steps to improve their disposable income. Of young married-couple families, 14 percent were reported receiving welfare assistance in the past three years, compared with only 3.5 percent of the elderly; 18 percent of these young families had moved into less costly housing (cf. 3.6 percent of the elderly); 30 percent of them had received financial help from kin (cf. 1.7 percent of the elderly); and in 42 percent of young married-couple families someone had found an extra job (cf. 1.9 percent of the elderly).

The 12 Winnipeg Area Study questions about the different strategies that people may take in order to cope with a period of financial difficulty can be combined into an index of financial stress. Comparisons of average levels of financial stress between households at the extremes are striking (see Table 8.2). Winnipeg survey data show clearly that the most stressed families are the ones with young children, whereas the elderly have the least financial stress. Although many old people are far from being

TABLE 8.2
Mean Financial Stress among Families, Winnipeg, 1988

Household Type	Stress Index	Standard Deviation
Sole-parent Family[a]	(5.1)	(2.8)
One Person, Age <45	3.3	2.7
Married Couple, Husband's Age <45, Child <5	4.1	2.7
Married Couple, Husband's Age <45, Child 5-17	2.3	2.1
Married Couple, Husband's Age <45, No Children	2.7	2.1
One Person, Age 45-64	(2.7)	(2.6)
Married Couple, Husband's Age 45-64, Child <18	3.0	2.6
Married Couple, Husband's Age 45-64, No Children	1.4	1.9
Elderly, Age 65+[b]	0.9	1.7

[a]Includes one adult and her/his children under age 18.
[b]Includes one person age 65+ or married couple, husband's age 65+.
( ) Indicates cell is <30 cases.

affluent, and some of them experience financial constraint, it appears that most of the elderly today have a level of financial security which exceeds that of the younger generations.

DISCUSSION

This chapter has addressed the controversial issue of intergenerational inequity, from a life course perspective. Economic life chances at different ages have been compared, and the outcome is clear. Childhood is the worst stage of life, especially for children living in the United States. The age distribution of income and wealth in North America is arguably the most striking of the new forms of poverty described in this book. In the past, temporal variations in life chances were due mainly to life cycle fluctuations in family responsibilities, relative to the resources of family heads. Today, there is a life course gradient of declining incidence of poverty with increasing age, which has created large differences in well-being between the young and the old.

Economic differences between the young and the old raise troubling questions about intergenerational equity (Moon, 1993). The core idea in the concept of intergenerational equity is the ideal that all age groups should have equal life chances. In a weaker sense, it includes the idea that any inequalities between the age groups should at least take the form of unsystematic fluctuations. Finding systematic inequalities between children and the elderly challenges the assumption that all generations are treated equally, and it calls into question the private and public choices that have altered the age profile of well-being (Preston, 1984).

At the end of the nineteenth century and in the first half of the twentieth century, the elderly were a poverty-stricken section of the population. After World War II, a long economic boom made it possible to increase public pensions and other programs for the elderly in order to bring their poverty rate down. It must have seemed to many policy makers then that intergenerational inequalities were on their way to being solved. Constantly rising real wages enabled almost all families with working-age heads to improve their standards of living. At the same time, most families were able to pay the increased taxes to fund public transfers of income for those who were not working and not earning. The elderly, who began to withdraw from regular employment at younger ages, were the primary beneficiaries of the expanded income transfers provided by the welfare state.

In contrast to public support for the elderly, there has been less support for subsidizing families with children in the Anglo-Saxon countries, and what little support there has been is now wilting under the pressure to cut government expenditures, which is justified by claims that families should take more responsibility for themselves. Family life in North America is currently in the throes of deregulation. Institutional supports for families are often being dismantled by public policies that neglect women, children, and families (Allen & Baber, 1992). Children and their parents are losing political influence, and young families in particular have experienced an erosion of public support (Wolfe, 1991). In Canada, this includes the recent elimination of Family Allowances, which had been paid to all families with children for over forty years. We need to understand the political economy of family deregulation today and its implications for inequality, because it has important implications for the emerging struggle for intergenerational equity between the young and the old (Kingson & Williamson, 1991).

Until recently, publicly organized economic improvements for the elderly raised few questions about intergenerational injustice. The assumption was that economic growth, combined with the redistribution of incomes by the state, would make it possible for everyone to be better off. Today, in the absence of steady economic growth, and with stagnant or falling real wages, economic conditions are no longer improving for everyone. Although the elderly continue to receive their pensions, employment is often scarce and full-time jobs with decent wages are in short supply. As a result, the post–World War II political economy now seems to be creating serious injustices between the generations. It is therefore time to examine how the welfare state both alleviates *and* *creates* the social distribution of poverty at the end of the twentieth century.

NOTES

1.   In a study of the economic needs of working-class people in the 1930s, Rowntree stated firmly, "It is normal for men to marry and to have to support families, and provision should accordingly be made for this when fixing minimum wages. It is not normal for women to have to support dependents" (Rowntree, 1937, p. 105). Rowntree consistently viewed women's wages, together with children's wages, as supplementary earnings.

2.   In the Canadian Family Expenditure Survey public use file, the highest age group recorded is age 76 or older. It is therefore not possible to identify individuals in extreme old age for this sample.

3.   The conclusion that qualifying for pension income actually lifts some people out of poverty has also been drawn from Family Expenditure Survey data for the United Kingdom. In a financial analysis of the "third age," people aged 50 to 74, Paul Johnson reports, "Surprisingly the very poorest are not the oldest but rather those under pension age who are not in work and not entitled to the higher benefits payable to pensioners" (1992, p. vii).

4.   The pattern of expenditure cuts for sole-parent families in Winnipeg is more extreme than it is for married-couple families with children. However, the number of sole-parent families in the Winnipeg Area Study is small, and the results are not reported here, since data on individual questionnaire items may be considered unreliable.

9

Shifting Entitlements

The modern state plays a major role in the social organization of consumption (Rein & Rainwater, 1988). Government intervention, which is intended to alter the market distribution of well-being, often produces different effects on different sections of the population. The result may be to create consumption cleavages between groups that receive unequal state benefits and that make unequal contributions to the costs of the state (Saunders, 1986).

One possible source of consumption cleavage is the tendency for taxation and income transfer policies to favor individuals in the later stages of the life course (Cheal, 1995). Efforts to measure accurately the economic status of the elderly relative to the nonelderly, taking into account taxes and transfers, have shown that the elderly enjoy a more favorable position than groups such as households headed by women (Danziger, van der Gaag, Smolensky, & Taussig, 1984; Danziger & Weinberg, 1994). In the United States, the adjusted disposable income of the elderly is 88 percent higher than the income of sole-parent families (Smeeding, Torrey, & Rein, 1988). It seems that the modern state has helped to organize an unequal temporal distribution of life chances (Thomson, 1989a).

In recent decades, programs serving children and their families have grown more slowly than other programs in both the United States and Canada (Bane, Wilson, & Baer, 1980; Battle & Torjman, 1993). Spending on pensions, in particular, has increased very rapidly. This growth can be partly explained by an increase in the number of older people in recent years, but it is due mainly to a larger proportion of the elderly becoming eligible for benefits, and because the average level of benefits has improved. This can be demonstrated when the effect of population aging is controlled, by adjusting the amount spent on social security per capita. In the United States, per capita public spending on the elderly was three times as high as public spending on children in 1960, and it remained three times as high in 1979 (Bane, Boatright, & Baer, 1980). The tilt of social spending toward the elderly has increased in recent years. Between fiscal years 1978 and 1987, U.S. federal expenditures targeted on children declined by 4 percent in real terms; those targeting the elderly increased by 52 percent (Danziger & Weinberg, 1994). In Canada, spending on child benefits has remained essentially flat since the mid-1970s, while spending on pension benefits has jumped (Battle & Torjman, 1993). The available data suggest that there was a general switch of state priorities to pension spending from the mid-1970s through the 1980s, that was not simply a consequence of demographic pressures (O'Higgins, 1988).

UNEVEN CUTS

In recent years, governments have attempted to reduce their social expenditures by a combination of eliminating programs, raising eligibility requirements, and reducing benefit levels. No section of the population has been completely spared from these cuts. However, the impact of government spending controls has been uneven. The most serious cuts have often been made to programs that benefit unattached young adults and families with children (Battle, 1993). On the other hand, significant reductions in benefits for the elderly, such as the planned raising of the retirement age in the United States, have typically been postponed until sometime in the twenty-first century.

In an era in which public programs are increasingly scrutinized for potential cost savings, the elderly have tended to be saved harmless by being placed outside the parameters of policy reform. One way in which this occurs is that programs for the elderly may simply not be made visible in the same manner as other programs. Battle and Torjman (1993) have pointed out that in Canada federal government estimates of social spending generally exclude the cost of the Canada Pension Plan (CPP). There appears to be no fiscal logic to this exclusion. It might be argued that excluding CPP from social accounting is justified on the grounds that, although it is administered by the federal government, it is financed by payroll contributions from employees and their employers. However, the Canadian Unemployment Insurance program (UI), which is also administered by the federal government, and which is also financed by payroll deductions, is nevertheless included in the national accounts on social spending. The effect of such illogical treatment of related programs is to distort the processes of policy evaluation and reform.

The political consequences of the differential accounting treatment of CPP and UI have been striking. In late 1994, the Canadian Minister of Human Resources Development, Lloyd Axworthy, launched a process to reform social security programs under federal jurisdiction (Human Resources Development Canada, 1994). The triple focus of social reform was to be on programs concerning work (i.e., unemployment insurance and job finding), learning (i.e., education and training), and social assistance (i.e., income transfers for families in need). Old age protection was not even mentioned. Whereas UI was targeted for additional changes and cuts on top of those already implemented in previous years, any discussion of altering programs for the elderly was left to a later day.

Special treatment given to income-support programs for the aged has raised the suspicion that old people have an excess of political influence and that they use it to protect themselves from any shift in entitlement to public funding. According to this view, the growing percentage of old people means that the balance of power, and therefore the balance of interest, is shifting toward older age groups (Thomson, 1989b). In our aging welfare states, children may be in danger of becoming a "forgotten minority" (Richman & Stagner, 1986).

On the other hand, the elderly may be in danger of suffering from a backlash against their dependence on government transfers. The emergence of new patterns of poverty since the 1970s, which have not been solved by new government interventions, have left the elderly in a politically exposed position. According to Smolensky, Danziger, and Gottschalk: "Although government policy is primarily responsible for the recent decline in poverty among the elderly, [it is] the disappointing trend in the earnings of the parents of children — not reductions in government benefits — [that] is primarily responsible for rising poverty among children. Poverty among children also rose because of the increase in the percentage of all children living in single-parent families and the very high poverty rate of these families" (1988, p. 29–30).

Income-support programs for the elderly may need special protection, because cutting them would have very serious consequences. If the pretransfer needs of the elderly are relatively large, as seems to be the case (Weinberg, 1985), then the only alternative to massive transfer payments is a very high rate of poverty in old age. Without transfer payments, half of all Canadian elderly families would have been below Statistics Canada's low-income cut-offs (i.e., poverty line) in 1985 (Rashid, 1990c). The U.S. Bureau of the Census has calculated that the percentage of elderly U.S. residents in poverty in 1990 was 46.8 percent before government transfers but only 9.5 percent after all cash transfers and noncash transfers are included in income (U.S. Bureau of the Census, 1991). Viewed from one angle, this major reduction in post-transfer poverty among the aged is one of the great success stories of the modern welfare state (Neugarten & Neugarten, 1989). Viewed from another angle, government transfer programs in the United States have a smaller poverty reduction impact on sole-parent families than they do on the elderly. In 1990, the effect of government transfers on persons in families having a female householder with no husband present was to reduce the poverty rate of whites in this category from 45.6 percent to 30.3 percent. Among blacks in this family category in that year, government transfers reduced the poverty rate from 64.7 percent to 44.0 percent (U.S. Bureau of the Census, 1991).

The nature of intergenerational transfers and their relation to intergenerational equity is part of a larger set of questions about who gains the most from state income-support systems. Various aspects of this problem have been investigated in recent years (Hedström & Ringen, 1987; Smeeding, Torrey, & Rein, 1988; Mitchell, 1991; Danziger & Weinberg, 1994). Nevertheless, the effects of income policies are rarely examined in a comprehensive manner, with respect to the various types of households most at risk of being poor (though see Danziger, 1988). Comparisons of poverty rates with and without government intervention will therefore be conducted here, taking into account the findings on individuals and families in poverty reviewed in earlier chapters.

IMAGINE NO INTERGENERATIONAL REDISTRIBUTION

Governments seek to alleviate poverty by intervening in the distribution of income in two main ways, through taxes and transfers. Taxes and other payroll deductions reduce the flow of income into the household economy, by removing money from the income stream. Transfers increase the household income by providing additional cash. The balance of income deductions and income supplements or, in other words, net transactions with the state, determines the extent of the benefit, if any, that a household derives from public incomes policies.

In principle, individuals and families with high market incomes should pay heavier taxes than those with low market incomes, and people with low market incomes should receive more in public transfers than do individuals and families with high earnings and relatively large investment incomes. When the balance of income deductions and income transfers is taken into account, poor households should have positive net transactions with the state (i.e., they should be net recipients). Affluent households should have negative net transactions with the state (i.e., they should be net donors).

A critical issue for social policy is whether or not fiscal programs match social ideals. This raises questions about the effectiveness of antipoverty programs. It is also important to know whether or not all disadvantaged groups are treated fairly by income tax and income transfer policies. This is the question of equity in antipoverty programs.

Viewed from a life course perspective, an effective system of income redistribution should take money from age groups that are relatively well-off and give money to age groups that are relatively disadvantaged. If the income redistribution is also equitable, it should not increase the rate of poverty in groups that are net donors, nor should it give net recipient groups a better chance of avoiding poverty than net donor groups.

The first step in examining these issues is to remove from the calculation of household income all government deductions from income (i.e., taxes and payroll levies), together with all government additions to income other than the salaries and pensions earned by government employees (i.e., transfers). The resulting estimates of what income poverty would be like without government intervention are reported in Figures 9.1 and 9.2. For the purposes of these two figures, income poverty is defined as a level of income before transfers and taxes that is less than half the national median.

It is clear that without government support older persons over age 65 would be by far the poorest age group, in both the United States and Canada. Whether income is adjusted per capita or per reference equivalent makes no difference to this conclusion. A comparison of Figures 9.1 and 9.2 with Figures 8.2 and 8.3 shows that the intergenerational redistribution of income, from the working-age population to those who are retired, has been very effective in solving most of the problem of poverty at the end of the life course. Between two-fifths (United States)

FIGURE 9.1

**Avoiding Income Poverty Over the Life Course without
Government Intervention, United States, 1992**

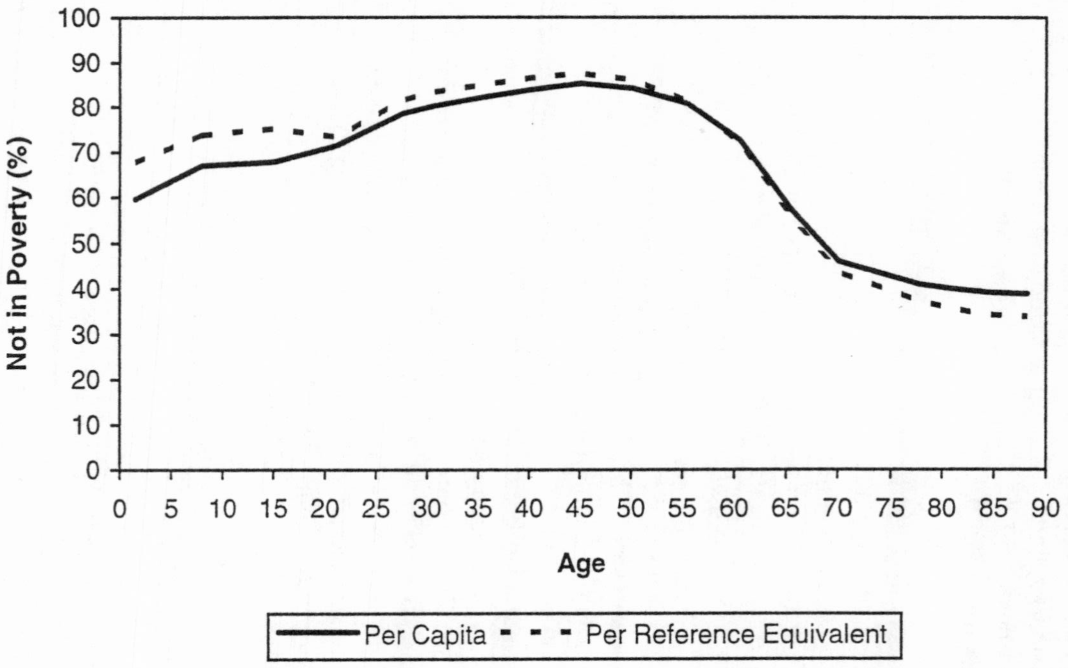

FIGURE 9.2

Avoiding Income Poverty Over the Life Course without Government Intervention, Canada, 1992

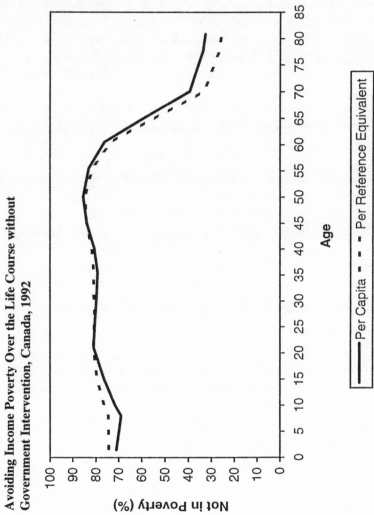

and three-fifths (Canada) of all elderly have been raised out of poverty by the combination of income taxation and transfers policies. That is a great improvement over the situation in England described by Rowntree in the mid-1930s (Rowntree, 1941).

In contrast to the striking effectiveness of income policies for the elderly, intergenerational equity is a more ambiguous issue. Among all Canadian and U.S. residents, the elderly have a better chance of avoiding income poverty per capita after redistribution than do the nonelderly. Comparisons of income poverty per reference equivalent, on the other hand, suggest that differences between the elderly and the nonelderly are not very great.

The most troubling finding with respect to intergenerational inequity concerns children in the United States (see also Sharif & Phipps, 1994). Here, young children have an absolutely smaller chance of avoiding income poverty per capita after redistribution than before redistribution. Before government intervention, 40.4 percent of U.S. children under age four have money incomes per capita that are less than half the national median. After all government income transfers and deductions have been applied, 46.3 percent of these children have less than half the national median income per capita. This outcome can only be described as perverse.

THE HEGEMONIC POOR AND THE OTHER POOR

Children and the elderly are both at risk of being poor. However, these two groups have received unequal attention. Whereas the economic problems of the elderly have been central to the North American version of the welfare state, the problems of young children have been pushed to the margins of society.

Societal solutions to the problem of poverty evolve through a political process. In that process, some groups are inevitably favored and others are disfavored. Selective policy emphases sometimes appear to be accidental, as when it is suggested that no one intended to bring about the recent shift in entitlements toward the elderly. At the same time, biases in program entitlements may also express values held by dominant groups about the contrast between the "deserving" poor and the "undeserving" poor. It is therefore worth exploring the forms of marginalization in poverty policy, to see if they follow any pattern.

We have seen that a number of vulnerable groups can be identified. Among these groups, three types of situations are of special interest.[1] The first type of situation is one in which vulnerable groups have a relatively low incidence of poverty, due to the fact that they benefit from large positive net transactions with the state. Such groups may be referred to as *well supported*. They may also be referred to as *hegemonic* groups, since they dominate the politics of income security at the expense of other groups whose needs are not well met. Second, there are groups that engage in positive net transactions with the state, but the transactions are modest and have only limited effectiveness in reducing their poverty. These groups are *weakly supported*. Finally, there is the situation in which relatively serious poverty not only is not alleviated but also is actually exacerbated by negative net transactions with the state. Groups in this situation are evidently *marginalized*. The Consumer Expenditure Survey for the United States and the Family Expenditure Survey for Canada permit identifying groups within the above three categories of state support, according to the following criteria.

Weakly supported and well supported groups together are distinguished from marginalized groups by the fact that the former two categories have positive balances in net transactions with the state, whereas the latter category has a negative balance in net transactions.

The weakly supported and well supported groups are distinguished from each other by the amount of their positive net transactions with the state, adjusted per capita and per reference equivalent. Weakly supported groups are those in which the average annual net transaction with the state is less than +$5,000 per capita, or less than +$7,000 per reference equivalent. Well supported groups are those whose favorable balance with the state exceeds these figures.

The well supported groups are distinguished from the weakly supported and marginalized groups by the fact that the latter two categories have rates of income poverty that are far above the national norm, whereas the former category does not. Here it is necessary to take account of the different welfare regimes in Canada and in the United States. There is a large difference between these countries in the incidence of poverty that is statistically normal, and different standards are therefore needed to define what constitutes marginalization in the two societies. For present purposes, an income poverty rate is considered to be high in Canada if it exceeds 15 percent of the group, and it is considered to be high in the United States if it exceeds 35 percent. Below these levels, the rate of poverty is considered to lie within the range of normal experience for the particular country.

Well supported, weakly supported, and marginalized groups in the United States and Canada are listed below. Each listing provides the group's sociodemographic characteristics, the direction and size of the average net transaction with the state for members of that group, and the relative frequency of the group whose total receipts after all deductions are less than half the national median. As usual, all financial statistics have been calculated two ways, with adjustments per capita and per reference equivalent.

U.S. Consumer Unit Financial Statistics

Well Supported Groups
Per Capita:
> Reference person age 65–74 (net +$5,570; 11.2 percent poor)
> Reference person age 75 or over (net +$6,828; 8.9 percent poor)
> Unmarried woman age 65 or over living alone (net +$7,258; 6.9 percent poor)

Per Reference Equivalent:
> Reference person age 65–74 (net +$7,176; 17.2 percent poor)
> Reference person age 75 or over (net +$7,626; 23.7 percent poor)
> Unmarried woman age 65 or over living alone (net +$7,258; 26.9 percent poor)

Weakly Supported Groups
Per Capita:
> Female sole parent (net +$462; 62.1 percent poor)
> Reference person under age 65, not employed (net +$2,073; 54.2 percent poor)

Per Reference Equivalent:
> Female sole parent (net +$766; 55.4 percent poor)
> Reference person under age 65, not employed (net +$3,618; 57.6 percent poor)

Marginalized Groups
Per Capita:
> Children present, including ages under 13 (net –$637; 37.8 percent poor)
> Large family, three or more children (net –$250; 57.3 percent poor)
> Reference person under age 65, full-year wage worker at low wage (net –$603; 36.2 percent poor)
> Couple under age 65, neither partner full-year wage workers (net –$12; 40.0 percent poor)
> Couple under age 65, husband-breadwinner/wife-homemaker with children (net –$989; 35.1 percent poor)
> Reference person age 18–24 (net –$516; 42.8 percent poor)

Per Reference Equivalent
    Large family, three or more children (net –$547; 39.8 percent poor)
    Reference person age 18–24 (net –$614; 47.4 percent poor)

Canadian Household Financial Statistics

Well Supported Groups
Per Capita:
    Reference person age 65–74 (net + $6,984; 3.1 percent poor)
    Reference person age 75 or over (net + $7,686; 2.7 percent poor)
    Unmarried woman age 65 or over living alone (net + $9,185; 1.7 percent poor)
Per Reference Equivalent:
    Reference person age 65–74 (net + $9,023; 8.1 percent poor)
    Reference person age 75 or over (net + $9,223; 10.3 percent poor)
    Unmarried woman age 65 or over living alone (net +$9,185; 14.3 percent poor)

Weakly Supported Groups
Per Capita:
    Female sole parent (net +$2,107; 35.1 percent poor)
    Reference person under age 65, not employed (net +$3,624; 24.8 percent poor)
    Couple under age 65, neither partner full-year wage workers (net +$1,091; 20.5 percent poor)
Per Reference Equivalent:
    Female sole parent (net +$3,502; 30.8 percent poor)
    Reference person under age 65, not employed (net +$5,749; 31.0 percent poor)

Marginalized Groups:
Per Capita:
    Children present, including ages under 13 (net –$1,756; 18.2 percent poor)
    Large family, three or more children (net –$1,142; 34.7 percent poor)
Per Reference Equivalent:
    Large family, three or more children (net –$2,491; 16.2 percent poor)
    Reference person not married, under age 65 (net –$1,400; 18.3 percent poor)
    Reference person single adult, i.e., never married and living independently, under age 65 (net –$2,588; 20.5 percent poor)
    Reference person age 18–24 (net –$630; 16.8 percent poor)

Financial statistics on consumer units in the United States and on households in Canada show that not all of the poor are treated in the same way. The only vulnerable people who are relatively well supported by the state are the elderly. That is true for the United States and for Canada, and regardless of whether income is adjusted per capita or by an equivalence scale. In light of the attention that continues to be paid to the plight of elderly women (Thomas, 1994), it is remarkable to find that they are neither marginalized nor weakly supported. The most vulnerable of these women, namely those who are unmarried and living alone, are nevertheless well supported in comparison with poverty groups among the nonelderly.

At the other end of the scale, the characteristics of groups that are marginalized reflect national differences in policy regimes between the United States and Canada. More U.S. groups are marginalized when income poverty is calculated per capita (6 to 2), and more Canadian groups are marginalized when income poverty is calculated per reference equivalent (4 to 2). This difference appears to be due to neglect of unmarried persons without children in Canada and to lack of support in the United States for working families that have children in need and low earnings.

Despite these interesting differences in the nature of marginalization between the United States and Canada, there are also important similarities between them. When income poverty is measured per capita, families containing children under age 13 and large families with three or more children are found to be marginalized in both countries. When income poverty is measured on the equivalence scale, large families are once again found to be marginalized in both the United States and Canada, together with reference persons aged 18–24. The fact that large families are marginalized in both countries, no matter how income poverty is measured, is dramatic proof of the extent to which this group has been shut out of the policy-making process. In addition, the fact that families with children as well as young adults are marginalized seems to confirm the thesis of intergenerational inequity in contemporary welfare states. A comparison of the well supported groups with the marginalized groups reveals some sharp contrasts in the political economies of different generations.

Between the poles of relatively strong state support and lack of state support are the weakly supported groups. Here, too, there are similarities and differences between Canada and the United States, but the similarities are more prominent. Female sole parents and the nonelderly who are not employed are groups whose vulnerability is officially recognized. However, they do not receive enough support to keep almost all of them out of poverty.

Some of the highest rates of income poverty are found among female sole parents and the unemployed, despite the financial benefits they receive. There are two ways of looking at this situation. On the one hand, it may be claimed that the level of government support provided has clearly been inadequate, and it should therefore be increased. On the other hand, it can be argued that state support has clearly failed to help these people climb out of poverty, and therefore programs directed at sole parenthood and at unemployment should be changed. In a climate of increasing fiscal conservatism, when politicians want to save large amounts of money from government programs, sole parents and the unemployed are not only economically vulnerable but are also politically vulnerable. They are prime targets for benefit cuts and social reengineering.

Political support for cuts to programs benefiting sole parents and the unemployed can be expected from high-income earners in the United States and Canada. The latter groups dislike the way in which the value of their incomes has eroded in recent years, and they hope to reverse that trend through income tax cuts. Opposition to special benefits for unmarried mothers and the able-bodied unemployed may also come from some marginalized groups. These groups are unlikely to appreciate why a particular social category with a high rate of poverty is financially supported by people like themselves, when they too have trouble making ends meet.

POLITICAL ECONOMY OF CHILDREN
AND THE ELDERLY

Some of the most marginalized families in the United States and Canada today are large families. This is ironic, in view of the public importance that politicians on both sides of the border seem to attach to "family values." It is common to hear policy makers claim that the family is the basis of our society and that the changes they want are "for our children," yet the families in which children are most important receive little recognition.

Large families in many ways exemplify the traditional family values of marriage, children, and caring for dependents. Most large families are two-parent families. In the United States, 71.8 percent of reference persons in large families are married, and in Canada 85.5 percent are married. The average (mean) number of children under age 18 in large families is 3.3 in Canada and 3.6 in the United States. Almost all (97 percent) of the large families in both countries contain one or more children under age 13.

Working to maintain the family is an important value for the heads of most large families. In the United States, 74.5 percent of reference persons in large families were either fully employed (54.9 percent) or partially employed for more than two weeks during 1992. In Canada, 80.7 percent were so employed (51.5 percent full-time).

Large families headed by a married couple almost always engage in employment of some form. Only 7.0 percent of U.S. couples with large families had neither spouse employed for more than two weeks in 1992, and a mere 4.3 percent of Canadian couples with large families engaged in no significant paid employment. Couples with three or more children do, however, differ from other married couples in their inability, or unwillingness, to practice full-time employment by both spouses. One partner, typically the wife, is usually either a full-time or part-time care-giver for the children. Under one-fifth (19.4 percent) of Canadian couples with three or more children are dual-career couples, and just 16.2 percent of U.S. couples with large families are dual-career couples.

Large families do not have high overall labor force participation rates. That is partly because child rearing is a labor-intensive activity and partly because of the heavy financial cost of purchasing daycare for several children at once. It is not surprising, then, that many of these families have economic difficulties in the absence of government support. What is more noteworthy is that so few of these families receive significant public support, not only in the United States but also in Canada.

In both the United States and Canada, a little over one-third of all large families have positive net transactions with the state (37.9 percent in the United States and 35.8 percent in Canada). Most large families pay more to governments than they get in return. On average (median), large families in the United States make net contributions to the state of $1,377 per year. Large families in Canada pay $6,000 more per year in taxes and other levies than they receive in transfers.

It is interesting to compare the political economy of large families with that of the elderly aged 65–74 (i.e., the young-old). In both Canada and the United States, 88 percent of families with a reference person age 65–74 benefit from positive net transactions with the state. The median annual value of net transactions with all governments for the families of the young-old in the United States in 1992 was +$8,735. For the families of the young-old in Canada, the median net transaction with the state was

+$10,496. Benefits of this size are not likely to be given up willingly, nor easily.

DISCUSSION

In this chapter, the role of the state in setting income-support policies for different groups has been studied in detail. The results show that governments in the United States and Canada both decrease the risk of poverty and increase the risk of poverty, for different groups. The only vulnerable groups that are well supported by the state in both countries are the elderly. Marginalized groups are more diverse, but they tend to cluster at the other end of the life course. Some of these groups that have above-average numbers of poor people suffer large deficits in their net transactions with the state, especially in Canada. Governments in Canada and the United States have the capacity to alter market distributions of income in pursuit of their social policies. Saving the elderly from poverty is one of the oldest of those policies. Today, new policies that will alter the pattern of intergenerational entitlements to income support seem to be needed.

The drastic difference in public treatment between large families and the young-old would not matter if the result were to achieve parity between the two groups. However, that is not the case. Large families have poverty rates ranging from twice as much (per reference equivalent) to five times as much or more (per capita) than households and consumer units with a reference person age 65–74. Surely it is one of the sadder paradoxes of postmodern politics that the welfare state is involved in creating an inequality of this sort.

NOTE

1. There is a fourth type of situation that is not discussed in the chapter text, because it is deemed to be of lesser interest. That situation involves groups having some poverty but lacking large positive net transactions with the state because their needs are relatively small. These groups may be referred to as *minor clients* of the welfare state. The net government transactions of minor clients of the Canadian and U.S. welfare states, whose poverty rates range from 12 to 15 percent in Canada and 28 to 35 percent in the United States, may be of some interest.

U.S. Consumer Unit Financial Statistics

Per Capita:

Reference person under age 65, part-year wage worker (net –$447; 34.2 percent poor)

Reference person not married, under age 65 (net –$778; 28.6 percent poor)

Per Reference Equivalent:

Reference person under age 65, part-year wage worker (net –$616; 32.8 percent poor)

Reference person under age 65, full-year wage worker at low wage (net –$884; 32.9 percent poor)

Reference person not married, under age 65 (net –$970; 32.3 percent poor)

Reference person single adult, under age 65 (net –$1,329; 32.0 percent poor)

Couple, under age 65, neither partner full-year wage worker (net –$20; 30.1 percent poor)

Canadian Household Financial Statistics

Per Capita:

Couple under age 65, husband-breadwinner/wife-homemaker with children (net –$2,201; 14.1 percent poor)

Reference person age 18–24 (net –$496; 14.8 percent poor)

Per Reference Equivalent:

Couple, under age 65, neither partner full-year wage worker (net +$1,798; 13.8 percent poor)

10

The Postmodernization of Poverty

Old people and children have benefited unequally from economic and political change in the twentieth century. At the beginning of the century, the early years of life were associated with a high risk of poverty. Children still have an above-average risk of being poor today. In contrast, the elderly, who experienced great absolute poverty at the beginning of the century, and extreme relative poverty in the middle of the century, have fared much better. Comparatively low rates of poverty among the elderly in the 1990s are dramatic proof of the positive benefits of targeted income transfer programs. The fact that children have not benefited from the modern welfare state in the same way raises some interesting questions.

The idea that the welfare state could be responsible for creating economic inequalities would have seemed preposterous to the early social reformers, yet we have seen that it is an idea that must be taken seriously today. It is a challenging idea, because it calls into question assumptions about progress and about the beneficial role of the state in economic and social development.

In the first chapter of this book, several theories of modernization were reviewed, and their implications for understanding the phenomenon of poverty were outlined. It is now time to reexamine those theories in light of our research findings.

Modernization theorists are essentially committed to the ideal that improvement in people's chances of leading a full and happy life is a dominant cultural value of modern societies. Providing a minimum subsistence income for everyone and equalizing the risk of relative poverty between different social groups are believed to be important goals in the attempt to realize that value. Furthermore, modernization theorists believe that individual and collective management of the risk of poverty is possible, to a greater or lesser extent. The means for achieving this include the invention of new technologies, new forms of social organization, and new codes of conduct. Where the various theorists of modernization differ is in their assessment of what has actually been achieved thus far and in their judgment of where the barriers to further progress lie. Standard modernization theorists, critical modernization theorists, and radical modernization theorists all draw distinctly different pictures of modern society and the place of poverty within it.

In this final chapter, evidence for and against the above three theories will be reviewed, drawing on findings from the empirical analyses reported earlier in the book. A case can be made for each of the theories. However, their cumulative limitations cast doubt on the value of continuing to study poverty as a consequence of imperfect modernization. Rather, it will be argued that a different conceptual framework is needed, namely one that is provided by postmodernization theory.

THE STANDARD MODERN VIEW OF POVERTY

Standard modernization theory takes a relatively unproblematic view of modern institutions and the environments that they create for families. It assumes that modern societies provide abundant opportunities for families to exploit. The only serious question, then, is how families can best utilize the opportunities open to them. The conventional answer to that question is that family members should pool their resources and provide each other with social supports.

Family members give and receive many kinds of supports. They share housing accommodations and assist in the tasks of daily living; they help other members get jobs; they provide financial reserves against loss of employment; they provide home care for the sick; and they help each other in myriad other ways. Through their giving and receiving of support, family members maximize the benefits derived from limited resources, and they provide some protection against risks. In a dynamic, market economy, social supports help to buffer families against the risk of poverty.

Viewed in this way, the vulnerability of some families to falling into poverty is due to transformations in family structure, which have the effect of weakening family ties. Loose family structures are characteristic of modern societies, due to the voluntaristic nature of personal relationships, as well as to the diffusion of interaction through amorphous social networks that exist in urban populations. Furthermore, the major rewards in a modern society are derived from occupational achievements, rather than from the performance of ascribed roles such as are found in traditional family structures. As a result, the strength of family ties depends on the internal dynamics of family life, which are largely beyond the control of public institutions.

Standard modern concerns about dysfunctional families have gone through three phases. During the 1950s and 1960s, the main area of concern about weak family supports was the common belief that extended family ties were becoming looser. It was feared that this could result in the impoverishment and neglect of the elderly who live alone. Peter Townsend (1957) allayed some of those fears with his study of the family life of old people in Bethnal Green, London. He found that elderly persons who belonged to localized extended families received a variety of supports. This included limited financial assistance, which prevented some of them from falling into poverty. Nevertheless, he cautioned that retired people were vulnerable who did not have local extended families or whose relatives could not afford to give much help. Townsend concluded that a small minority of the elderly were in dire poverty, or they were made only moderately poor rather than being very poor, because of small contributions from relatives.

In the following decades, fears about weakening family ties shifted to focus on marriage breakdown. The main economic issue here is the fact that female-headed families typically experience a large drop in income after divorce (Levitan, Belous, & Gallo, 1988; Conway, 1990). There is special concern about the vulnerability of dependent children, who usually remain with the mother when their parents separate.

Standard modern fears about declining family functioning have recently entered into a third phase. There is a growing concern about the possibility of less public support for the elderly in the future, due to current low birth rates in many western countries. The work of Kingsley Davis in the 1980s (1984; 1987) reflects this new interest of standard modernization theory. According to Davis, contemporary demographic shifts are due largely to the lack of control that kinship groups have over their members and, in particular, over women. Today, women have more incentive to engage in paid employment and less incentive to produce children for their kinsmen. The consequences of this change in women's motivations are a reduction in fertility, ultimately to a point below the population replacement level, and the aging of the population of the advanced industrial nations.

Projections of population aging have led financial analysts to point repeatedly to the long-term implications of declining fertility for the cost structures of modern welfare states. Increasing numbers of elderly dependents, combined with shrinking labor forces, are believed to pose a serious challenge for meeting the financial burden of age-related health and welfare programs early in the next century (Heller, Hemming, & Kohnert, 1986; Organization for Economic Cooperation and Development, 1988).

The research conducted for this book shows that there is a very significant body of evidence that is consistent with standard modernization theory. Much of that evidence has been presented in earlier chapters, both for the elderly who are not poor and for sole-parent families who are.

Most old people are not poor today. However, that is not because they receive substantial income support from their extended families. On the contrary, expenditure survey data show that the elderly are not significant net beneficiaries of interfamily transactions. In Chapter 8, we saw that in Winnipeg it is extremely rare for the elderly to receive financial help from kin.[1] The only reason why more of the elderly are not poor is the existence of substantial public income-support programs. In Chapter 9, striking evidence was presented to show how the economic situation of the elderly would deteriorate if all government intervention in income distribution ceased. Data on the relative contributions to income supports of the elderly from private and public transfers are consistent with a standard modern account of the declining economic relevance of extended families and the looming crisis of public transfer programs.

Likewise, the data on the severity of poverty in sole-parent families supports the idea that the greatest personal financial difficulties in our societies today are often due to a decline in traditional arrangements for income pooling. The legally regulated system of private social security provided within a moral economy of significant personal relationships clearly does not work in the way that it once did. When marriages break down, mothers often struggle to get by on their own. The disadvantages of very limited income sharing quickly become apparent in most cases.

Finally, it is worth making an often overlooked point about the relevance of standard modernization theory for explanations of contemporary poverty. Some of the most intractable cases of poverty today occur as a result of the combination of weak ties of affinity (e.g., marriage) and descent. In the absence of income pooling within marriage, it is conceivable that sole-support mothers could solve the worst of their financial problems by moving in with their kin, to form extended-family households. Indeed, the formation of complex households after marital disruption does occur. However, that arrangement is not common when separated or divorced women form households in which they are the family heads (see Chapter 4, n.2). Most separated or divorced female reference persons live without another adult present, other than an unmarried adult child. As a result, they do not benefit from significant sharing of household expenses, and inevitably many of them experience great financial stress.

Since standard modernization theory appears to be so obviously relevant to the analysis of contemporary family issues, one may wonder why any alternative theories should exist. There are two reasons for the existence of other theories of poverty. One reason is that it is not clear that the standard modern explanation given for what has been happening to families in fact identifies the correct cause. The other reason is that the account of poverty provided by standard modernization theory is incomplete.

The standard modern explanation for the weakening of family ties in modernity is that achievement values, and especially occupational achievements, have replaced ascribed family roles as central life interests. As a result, people are said to be less inclined to put family life first and more inclined to pursue economic opportunities open to them as individuals. That explanation may work well as an account of the declining significance of kinship ties, but it does not provide an entirely convincing account of increased numbers of sole-parent families.

After separating from their husbands, many women have fewer financial resources than they did when they were married. In addition, as noted in Chapter 4, previously married women are no more likely than currently married women to be in the labor force. This hardly suggests that there are many women who give up their marriages in order to pursue occupational success and financial freedom. Of course, it is possible that the decision to leave the marriage was not made by women at all, but by their husbands. Perhaps modern men are in search of more independent lifestyles, including greater control over their earnings. If that were the case, then the standard modern explanation for the growing numbers of sole-parent families would make sense. However, the assumption that all, or the overwhelming majority, of marital separations are the results of decisions made solely by husbands would be extreme. It seems unlikely that recent family changes can be explained simply as consequences of changing values among modern men, or women.

The second difficulty with standard modernization theory is that it does not pay enough attention to the failure of traditional income pooling arrangements to keep everyone out of poverty. Chapters 6 and 7 contain detailed analyses of family work systems and the income pools that are produced from them. It was clearly shown there that marriage gives no guarantee of protection against poverty. A couple must have either one member employed for a full year at a high wage, or both members employed — at least one of whom is employed full-year at a medium wage — before they will have a negligible chance of being poor. Couples in which neither partner is employed full-year are overrepresented in the poorest quintile of income and expenditure. Such findings lead to the conclusion that problems in modernity involve more than just weak family ties.

Standard modernization theory is the only significant theoretical approach today that takes "the family" to be the basic unit of society. As such, it is concerned with the functions performed by families and the preservation of the family as an enduring social form. All of the other theoretical approaches in the current discourse of modernity take the individual to be the unit of analysis. That is partly because, as more people move into and out of marriage, and between multiple families, the normal family life cycle explains less and less about individuals' life course trajectories. Recognition of that fact is an explicit assumption in critical modernization theory.

THE CRITICAL MODERN VIEW OF POVERTY

Critical modernization theory views modern society as a differentiated set of fields of opportunities and risks. In each field the individual is faced with the necessity of making choices. Any opportunity that is available involves certain risks that events will not turn out as planned. In a sense, everyone is a gambler in late modern society. Nobody can control all of the conditions on which her or his life depends, and accurate prediction is often hard or impossible. Viewed in this way, the poor are those who have gambled and lost.

Two fields of opportunities and risks are especially important in the critical modern view of poverty, namely, employment and personal relationships. In the latter field, marriage clearly entails certain risks, for men and women alike. However, the fragility of marital and family supports today poses special risks for women. They may find themselves without the support of a husband, even though they have heavy financial responsibilities for children. Divorce is the trap-door through which women fall into the new poverty, according to Ulrich Beck (1992, p. 89). Freedom to choose about personal relationships, and everything else, "frees" women to be poor.

In the labor market, the problem of poverty in the "risk society" is associated especially with the hazard of being unemployed. Like other risks, the probability of unemployment is socially distributed. Beck (1992) argues that risks of unemployment and poverty are hierarchically distributed, according to level of occupational skill. However, that may change with the computerization of white-collar work and the downsizing of many offices.

From the perspective of critical modernization theory, poverty is deemed to be largely the result of increasing instability in all areas of life, due to the accelerating pace of change. Driven by the worldwide extension of market competition and philosophies of continuous improvement, not only is change a constant feature of modern societies but also the speed of change is increasing. As the pace of change becomes faster, organizations and individuals adjust by adopting more flexible procedures that allow for a greater variety of inputs. They also enter into more temporary arrangements that permit the rapid reallocation of commitments and resources. Both types of adjustments create increased risks for clients, employees, and spouses, who may also have to adjust their behavior and their expectations.

Within organized institutions, results of accelerated change include increased turnover of the labor force and greater variability in patterns of work. At the individual level, these effects show up as more unemployment, more part-time work, and other "irregular" work practices. Within personal relationships, results include the replacement of traditional loyalties with semi-contractual agreements, fewer long-term commitments to specific persons, and a greater willingness to break off old relationships and to replace them with new ones. Here, the effects are visible as increased divorce, more blended families (i.e., stepfamilies), more sole-parent families, and so on.

Clearly, critical modernization theory is a serious attempt to respond to new and emerging conditions in contemporary social life. Its description of modern social life as an expanding set of increasingly volatile risks has important things to tell us about how people live and work today. Critical modernization theory also seems to have a unique capacity to explain the "new poverty," which takes the form of a curious conjunction of increased family instability and increased employment instability. The fact that both shifts are happening at the same time is comprehensible when they are explained as part of a larger paradigm shift in social organization.

Furthermore, critical modernization theory draws our attention to the fact that some groups of people face greater uncertainties than others. Young adults, who are trying to establish their independent identities, including independent households, and who are attempting to negotiate entry into the labor force, are notable examples. They are especially likely to experience unstable relationships, as well as unstable employment patterns. Both of these experiences put them at risk. In Chapter 8 we noted that American youths in the group from age 18 to 24 are at a greater risk of being poor than would be expected from the life course gradient of poverty. Similarly, in Chapter 6 we observed that single adults, who were younger than average, had a high rate of poverty. That was partly because they were less likely than older married adults to be fully employed during the early 1990s.

Critical modernization theory is obviously interesting, and relevant to many current concerns. However, it too seems unlikely to provide a comprehensive account of the social distribution of poverty. In particular, it remains unclear how much of the problem of children in poverty can be explained from a critical modern approach. Critical modern sociology has been most useful in analyzing the nature and consequences of individuals' life course choices, especially during young adulthood. Those analyses can be extended to include the ways in which children are affected by parents' choices, for instance about divorce and remarriage. Critical modernization theory would predict that increased instability in adult relationships will be accompanied by increased risk of poverty among children, unless children receive special protection from the state. What is not so evident is how far critical modernization theory can contribute to a better understanding of children as an underprivileged group.

The discourse of risk in critical modernization theory could no doubt be made broad enough to include the existential idea that simply being born exposes a child to certain risks. However, that does not seem to be a very useful approach for family sociology. Insofar as critical modernization theory has something distinctive to offer, beyond a statistical analysis of proportional hazards, it is the idea that freely chosen acts can have long-term consequences that are dangerous to the actor and to others. While the critical modern view of marriage may be an interesting way of looking at poverty among children of divorced parents, it does not seem to contribute much to understanding a systemic risk of poverty in childhood regardless of parental marital status. For an alternative approach with a clearer perspective on that issue, we may want to turn to radical modern theory.

THE RADICAL MODERN VIEW OF POVERTY

Radical modernization theory considers children to be a minority group (Qvortrup, 1991). The exclusion of children, as well as other minorities such as women, appears to be a side effect of a sorting process within modernization itself. In modernity, population categories are differentiated as inputs to the economic and political systems according to the resources they possess, the manner in which they utilize them, and the roles they are expected to perform. That process of differentiation has implications for the outputs that each group draws from its activities.

In principle, the exclusion of minority groups can take either of two forms — disorganized exclusion or organized exclusion. Disorganized exclusion is an outcome of the unseen hand of the market, as groups are selected or rejected according to their comparative uses under changing conditions. Here, the initial advantages of groups possessing greater resources often enable them to make better use of new opportunities. Groups that either are relatively lacking in resources or do not make the maximum use of them fall behind when commodity and labor markets change.

Economic exclusion can also take a more organized form. Here, groups that are deemed to be incapable of the normal levels of productivity expected in a technologically advanced economy are organized in special ways. That is done either in order to make them become more productive or in order to segregate them from the active centers of society with which they (presumably) cannot compete. At the extreme, the process of exclusion is completed by a cultural liquidation. The minority group is rendered practically invisible in the centers of power, due to its exclusion from official statistics. It has been argued that this is what has happened to children (Sgritta & Saporiti, 1989).

Illustrations of both organized and disorganized exclusion can be provided from the research materials presented in this book. Disorganized exclusion is probably best illustrated from Chapter 7. It was argued there that an economic regime of work intensification developed in North America over the last few decades. In a regime of work intensification, less work-intensive families are increasingly marginalized since the larger incomes of more work-intensive families enable them to dominate as buyers of goods and services. In a context of gender roles that accommodate and encourage working wives, married-couple families that do not have two full-year earners are likely to find themselves falling behind dual-career families. The former families therefore have an increased risk of falling into poverty.

A high risk of poverty due to organized exclusion would seem to be exemplified by the situation of children in Canada and the United States. The systemic nature of childhood poverty has been documented in Chapter 8. Despite the outpouring of lamentations about child poverty from leading public figures, the poverty of children is not accidental. It is the fixed position of children in a carefully graded system, in which the youngest children have the highest risk of poverty.

In truth, the economic experiences of children are partly organized and partly disorganized. Events such as birth into a family with several siblings, or marital separation by parents, are rarely socially organized. However, there is also an organized dimension to poverty among children that is orchestrated by the state.

In Chapter 9, the selectivity of the state in the amounts of income support for different families provided from government transfer programs and taxation policies was analyzed in detail. It was concluded that large families having three or more children are marginalized, in both the United States and Canada, regardless of how family income is adjusted for family size. When family income is adjusted per capita, all families containing children under age 13 are also found to be marginalized, in both countries. Both types of families can legitimately be described as excluded or marginalized. Despite having high rates of poverty, they have negative net transactions with the state (i.e., they send more dollars to the state than they receive from it).

Chapter 5 showed two reasons why the modern welfare states in North America have been successful in ignoring poor children. The first reason concerns the way in which data are often presented for use by policy makers. Poverty statistics, like a wide range of other microstatistics, are presented mainly at the family (or household) level. This procedure treats independent individuals, small families, and large families as equal units. Children in large families are therefore usually underpresented in official statistics and in the interpretations based on them. They have little visibility. Second, equivalence scales that are used by government departments to make judgments about families in need, and to set benefit levels for them, are weighted so as to minimize the needs of children.

The institutionalized mechanisms for the economic exclusion of children, and the consequences of those mechanisms, are intelligible. What is not so clear is why children are marginalized in the web of private and public entitlements,[2] although the elderly are not. Like children, older people have been excluded from the labor market, but most of the elderly have been compensated for the loss of employment by substantial income supports, whereas children have not. Children receive no financial compensation for the compulsory time that they must spend in school rather than working for wages.

Radical modernization theory would suggest that the difference between children and the elderly is that children have almost no power in the public sphere. The elderly, on the other hand, can vote, they have the time and (in many cases) the money to be politically active, and they tend to be well organized. From a radical modern point of view, the elderly have been able to bargain with employers and governments during the modernization of labor markets and the growth of the interventionist state. Old people have therefore exercised some control over the terms of their exclusion from gainful employment. Children, on the other hand, have had no such leverage.

Persuasive as these arguments are on behalf of radical modernization theory, there are still some unanswered questions. Although children themselves have had virtually no power in the public sphere, adults have sometimes acted in their (perceived) interests. From the nineteenth through the twentieth centuries, children's (socially constructed) interests have often been backed by social movements. Why were those movements not more successful in gaining permanent income security for children in the United States and Canada? Was that failure itself evidence of massive social exclusion of an undervalued minority?

Like critical modernization theory, the outer limits of radical modernization theory tend to fade into tautology. In this case, the tautological reasoning concerns the nature of minority status. In one sense, any group whose demands (or the demands made for them) are not recognized by the state may be labelled as a neglected minority. That is certainly a common enough political strategy these days, which can be very effective. However, the label of minority status in itself does not explain the position of a group within the political economy of the welfare state. If a minority group such as the disabled can gain wide sympathy and support, why not children? Why have we seemingly reached the limits of progress for children and the end of modernity's promise?

THE POSTMODERN VIEW OF POVERTY

At its most basic level, postmodernization theory is concerned with the fact that change in the most advanced western societies has reached a kind of impasse. Postmodernity appears as a new kind of chaos. It is not the kind of anomic chaos that is familiar to sociologists as the result of temporary social disorganization. As in modern societies, postmodern systems of meaning and action exist that are highly organized across time and space. The only difference is that in postmodernity the pieces of organized social life no longer fit together to form a functional unity.

In pluralistic, postmodern societies, the ideological deconstruction of once dominant ideas is practiced, and such ideas tend to lose their power to convince. As a result, individuals who are in a position to exercise power or influence often lack the absolute sense of conviction of their own rightness that is a prerequisite for imposing their way of life upon others. It is for this reason, the postmodernists argue, that intellectuals have given up attempting to legislate the details of people's lives (Bauman, 1987). Instead, they have encouraged a diminished role for the state and a relinquishing of its powers of compulsion. The consequence is a gradual deinstitutionalization of everyday life, in which both formal and informal social controls are loosened and in which the influence of reason and authority becomes more tentative and ambiguous.

Postmodern theories of change have tended to focus on the decline of reason and on the weakening of characteristically modern processes of rationalization, such as bureaucratization. This includes the suggestion that we are currently in a phase of widespread debureaucratization, in which managerial hierarchies are being replaced by more flexible market exchanges. Debureaucratization is a common feature of post-Fordist methods of industrial production. It also takes the form of the shrinking of the welfare state and the emergence of a post-welfare political agenda (Bennett, 1990; Crook, Pakulski, & Waters, 1992). One salient feature of postmodernity is the strengthening of market forces at the expense of the historically strong role of the nation state (Nowotny, 1993). The most obvious example of the shrinking of the state and the creation of a post-modern world order is the collapse of communism in eastern Europe and in Russia (Bauman, 1992). However, that is only the most dramatic example of a larger trend of the expansion of market transactions. Recommodification through the twin processes of the privatization of the public sector and the deregulation of the private sector has occurred in the western capitalist societies as well.

The modernization of western capitalism in the twentieth century saw the emergence of a "mixed economy," as a result of the rationalization of the relationship between individual interests represented by the market and the public interest represented by the state. In this symbiotic relationship the market economy provided the state with resources, mainly through the mechanism of taxation, and the state provided the market with planning (or "steering") as well as subsidies for social and technological risks. That arrangement is now breaking down, slowly in some places and more quickly in others.

As a result of the accumulation of fiscal deficits, failures of bureaucratic planning, negative effects of bureaucratic regulations, and intensified global competition, support for state intervention has fallen and the role of markets has grown. A predictable consequence of the shrinking of the welfare state and expanded market competition is an increase in economic inequality. The pluralization of lifestyles in postmodern societies is therefore accompanied by the polarization of incomes.

Furthermore, reappraisals of the role of the welfare state in contemporary group relations contribute to a growing sense that what contemporary welfare states produce is not so much social solidarity as forms of relative deprivation. A common difficulty in all modernization theories is their failure to give adequate recognition to imbalances and tensions in state income-support systems. The myth of the essentially beneficial role of the welfare state in income redistribution is a central component in the sociology of modernity. It is difficult to see how theories of the modernization of social life can be maintained once that myth is given up. The hypothesis is therefore advanced here that new configurations of poverty are due to a process of postmodernization.

Postmodernization is the process by which structures are made that do not fit together. The apparent intractability of the "new poverty" is one symptom of that process. Institutional levers to correct unwanted behaviors are either unavailable or ineffective, and the social programs that people had counted on to see them through hard times are being disassembled. The postmodernization of social programs gives an ironic twist to the modern invention of "social security." In the foundational policy discourse on risks in welfare states, institutions of social protection, such as pension plans and disability insurance plans, were proposed as means for managing the risks of living and working in modern societies (Ewald, 1983). Today, those institutions are often seen as powerful sources of risks themselves. That is because there is the possibility that unfunded liabilities will not be honored and the plans will collapse

(Repassy, 1990). The insecurity of social security is only one aspect of the postmodern world to which we are all learning to adjust. However, it is a factor that is potentially of critical significance for the poor.

The accumulation of unfunded liabilities in pay-as-you-go pension plans, and in a variety of other state programs, illustrates the manner in which postmodernity threatens to undermine standards of living in vulnerable groups. The underlying problem in the postmodernization of poverty is the tendency for modern institutions to be overloaded by multiple, inflationary expectations that cannot be met within available resources and techniques for program delivery. Whether the immediate cause of a particular imbalance is on the "demand" side or on the "supply" side is a historical question, to be determined in each case. The answers to specific questions of origination are less important than understanding why such imbalances are a general feature of postmodernity.

In postmodernity, there is a fundamental incompatibility in the structure of time between the dream of continuous improvement and the inevitable fluctuations in emotional, demographic, economic, and political environments. The result is a series of combinations of downside rigidities in entitlements and instabilities in the means for meeting them. These imaginary economies are accidents waiting to happen — and when accidents do happen, the consequences can be painful. Poverty is one of those consequences. If past experience is any guide, no one should expect the children to be saved.

NOTES

1.   It should be noted that the finding that the elderly in Winnipeg do not often receive financial help from kin is not due to some local peculiarity of social disorganization in kinship networks. Winnipeg is a demographically stable city, and it is the author's impression that in comparison with larger cities in North America, social life in Winnipeg is relatively family-centered.

2.   On the concept of standard of living as the product of a web of entitlements, see Sen (1981).

Bibliography

Allen, Katherine and Kristine Baber. 1992. "Starting a Revolution in Family Life Education." *Family Relations* 41: 378–84.

Axinn, June and Herman Levin. 1979. "The Family Life Cycle and Economic Security." *Social Work* 24: 540–46.

Axinn, June and Mark Stern. 1988. *Dependency and Poverty*. Lexington, Mass.: Lexington Books.

Baber, Kristine and Katherine Allen. 1992. *Women and Families*. New York: Guilford Press.

Baker, Maureen. 1994. "Thinking About Families: Trends and Policies." In *Canada's Changing Families*, edited by M. Baker, pp. 1–11. Ottawa, Ontario: Vanier Institute of the Family.

Bane, Mary Jo. 1986. "Household Composition and Poverty." In *Fighting Poverty: What Works and What Doesn't*, edited by S. Danziger and D. Weinberg, pp. 209–31. Cambridge, Mass.: Harvard University Press.

——. 1992. "Welfare Policy after Welfare Reform." In *Fulfilling America's Promise*, edited by J. Pechman and M. McPherson, pp. 109–28. Ithaca, N.Y.: Cornell University Press.

Bane, Mary Jo, Julie Boatright Wilson, and Neal Baer. 1980. "Trends in Public Spending on Children and Their Families." In *American Families and the Economy*, edited by R. Nelson and F. Skidmore, pp. 109–41. Washington, D.C.: National Academy Press.

Barlow, James and Simon Duncan. 1988. "The Use and Abuse of Housing Tenure." *Housing Studies* 3: 219–31.

Battle, Ken. 1993. "The Politics of Stealth." In *How Ottawa Spends: 1993–94*, edited by S. Phillips, pp. 417–48. Ottawa, Ontario: Carleton University Press.

Battle, Ken and Sherri Torjman. 1993. *Opening the Books on Social Spending*. Ottawa, Ontario: Caledon Institute of Social Policy.

Baudrillard, Jean. 1981. *For a Critique of the Political Economy of the Sign*. St. Louis, Mo.: Telos.

——. 1987. "Modernity." *Canadian Journal of Political and Social Theory* 11: 63–72.

Bauman, Zygmunt. 1987. *Legislators and Interpreters*. Ithaca, N.Y.: Cornell University Press.

——. 1992. *Intimations of Postmodernity*. New York: Routledge.

Beck, Ulrich. 1992. *Risk Society*. Newbury Park, Calif.: Sage.

Bennett, Robert. 1990. "Decentralization, Intergovernmental Relations and Markets." In *Decentralization, Local Governments, and Markets*, edited by R. Bennett, pp. 1–26. Oxford: Clarendon Press.

Berger, Brigitte and Peter Berger. 1983. *The War Over the Family*. Garden City, N.Y.: Doubleday.

Berger, Peter. 1977. *Facing Up To Modernity*. New York: Basic Books.

Bergmann, Barbara. 1986. *The Economic Emergence of Women*. New York: Basic Books.

Bianchi, Suzanne. 1993. "Children of Poverty." In *Child Poverty and Public Policy*, edited by J. Chafel, pp. 91–125. Washington, D.C.: Urban Institute Press.

Bird, Tom. 1990. "Shelter Costs." *Canadian Social Trends* 16: 6–10.

Blank, Rebecca and Alan Blinder. 1986. "Macroeconomics, Income Distribution, and Poverty." In *Fighting Poverty: What Works and What Doesn't*, edited by S. Danziger and D. Weinberg, pp. 180–208. Cambridge, Mass.: Harvard University Press.

Blank, Rebecca and Maria Hanratty. 1993. "Responding to Need: A Comparison of Social Safety Nets in Canada and the United States." In *Small Differences That Matter*, edited by D. Card and R. Freeman, pp. 191–231. Chicago: University of Chicago Press.

Blumstein, Philip and Pepper Schwartz. 1983. *American Couples: Money, Work, Sex*. New York: William Morrow.

Boh, Katja. 1989. "European Family Life Patterns — A Reappraisal." In *Changing Patterns of European Family Life*, edited by K. Boh, M. Bak, C. Clason, M. Pankratova, J. Qvortrup, G. Sgritta, and K. Waerness, pp. 265–98. New York: Routledge.

Booth, Charles. 1889. *Life and Labour of the People in London*. London: Williams and Norgate.

Bosch, Gerhard, Peter Dawkins, and François Michon. 1993. "Working Time in 14 Industrialised Countries." In *Times Are Changing*, edited by G. Bosch,

P. Dawkins, and F. Michon, pp. 1–45. Geneva: International Institute for Labour Studies.

Boudon, Raymond. 1986. *Theories of Social Change*. Berkeley: University of California Press.

Boyd, Monica and Edward Pryor. 1989. "The Cluttered Nest: The Living Arrangements of Young Canadian Adults." *Canadian Journal of Sociology* 14: 461–77.

Boyne, Roy and Ali Rattansi. 1990. "The Theory and Politics of Postmodernism." In *Postmodernism and Society*, edited by R. Boyne and A. Rattansi, pp. 1–45. Basingstoke: Macmillan.

Brannen, Julia and Peter Moss. 1987. "Dual Earner Households." In *Give and Take in Families*, edited by J. Brannen and G. Wilson, pp. 75–95. London: Allen and Unwin.

——. 1991. *Managing Mothers*. London: Unwin Hyman.

Britten, Rollo, J.E. Brown, and Isidore Altman. 1941. "Certain Characteristics of Urban Housing and their Relation to Illness and Accidents." In *Housing for Health*, edited by American Public Health Association, Committee on the Hygiene of Housing, pp. 159–81. Lancaster, Pa.: Science Press.

Brose, Hanns-Georg. 1989. "Coping With Instability — The Emergence of New Biographical Patterns." *Life Stories* 5: 3–25.

Buchmann, Marlis. 1989. *The Script of Life in Modern Society*. Chicago: University of Chicago Press.

Bunting, Trudi. 1991. "Social Differentiation in Canadian Cities." In *Canadian Cities in Transition*, edited by T. Bunting and P. Filion, pp. 286–312. Toronto, Ontario: Oxford University Press.

Burt, Martha. 1992. *Over the Edge*. New York: Russell Sage Foundation.

Canada Mortgage and Housing Corporation. 1994. "Low Income, Labour Force Participation and Women in Housing Need, 1991." *CMHC Research and Development Highlights* 16: 1–4.

Card, David and Richard Freeman. 1993. *Small Differences That Matter*. Chicago: University of Chicago Press.

Carden, Maren Lockwood. 1984. "The Women's Movement and the Family." *Marriage and Family Review* 7: 7–18.

Casper, Lynne, Sara McLanahan, and Irwin Garfinkel. 1994. "The Gender-poverty Gap." *American Sociological Review* 59: 594–605.

Cavan, Ruth Shonle. 1974. "Changes in Marriage and Family Life-Styles." In *Marriage and Family in the Modern World*, edited by R. S. Cavan, pp. 3–11. New York: Crowell.

Cheal, David. 1989. "Strategies of Resource Management in Household Economies." In *The Household Economy*, edited by R. Wilk, pp. 11–22. Boulder, Colo.: Westview Press.

——. 1990. "Social Construction of Consumption." *International Sociology* 5: 299–317.

——. 1991. *Family and the State of Theory*. Toronto, Ontario: Toronto University Press.

——. 1993a. "Unity and Difference in Postmodern Families." *Journal of Family Issues* 14: 5–19.

——. 1993b. "Changing Household Financial Strategies: Canadian Couples Today." *Human Ecology* 21: 197–213.

——. 1993c. "The Allocation of Labor in Marriage and Housing Resources." *Winnipeg Area Study Research Report*, No. 48. Winnipeg: University of Manitoba, Department of Sociology.

——. 1994. "Realism and Renewal in Family Theory." In *Family Sociology and Social Change*, edited by A. Leira, pp. 25–53. Oslo: Institute for Social Research.

——. 1995. "Repenser les transferts intergénérationnels." In *Les solidarités entre générations*, edited by C. Attias-Donfut, pp. 259–68. Paris: Nathan.

Che-Alford, Janet. 1990. "Home Ownership." *Canadian Social Trends* 16: 2–5.

Chisholm, Lynne and Manuela Du Bois-Reymond. 1993. "Youth Transitions, Gender and Social Change." *Sociology* 27: 259–79.

Clark, Susan, Frederick French, Margaret Dechman, and Burke MacCallum. 1991. *Mothers and Children*. Halifax: Nova Scotia Department of Community Services.

Coleman, Marilyn and Lawrence Ganong. 1989. "Financial Management in Stepfamilies." *Lifestyles: Family and Economic Issues* 10: 217–32.

Conway, John. 1990. *The Canadian Family in Crisis*. Toronto, Ontario: James Lorimer and Co.

Crompton, Rosemary and Michael Mann, eds. 1986. *Gender and Stratification*. Cambridge: Polity Press.

Crompton, Susan. 1994. "Left Behind: Lone Mothers in the Labour Market." *Perspectives on Labour and Income* 6(2): 23–28.

——. 1995. "Work and Low Income." *Perspectives on Labour and Income* 7(2): 12–14.

Crook, Stephen, Jan Pakulski, and Malcolm Waters. 1992. *Postmodernization*. London: Sage.

Currie, Raymond. 1988. "Selected Findings from the 1988 Winnipeg Area Study." *Winnipeg Area Study Research Report*, No. 24. Winnipeg: University of Manitoba, Department of Sociology.

Dahrendorf, Ralf. 1979. *Life Chances*. Chicago: University of Chicago Press.

Danes, Sharon and Mary Winter. 1990. "The Impact of the Employment of the Wife on the Achievement of Home Ownership." *The Journal of Consumer Affairs* 24: 148–69.

Danziger, Sheldon. 1988. "Recent Trends in Poverty and the Antipoverty Effectiveness of Income Transfers." In *The Distributional Impacts of Public Policies*, edited by S. Danziger and K. Portney, pp. 33–46. New York: St. Martin's Press.

Danziger, Sheldon, Jacques van der Gaag, Eugene Smolensky, and Michael Taussig. 1984. "Income Transfers and the Economic Status of the Elderly." In *Economic Transfers in the United States*, edited by M. Moon, pp. 239–82. Chicago: University of Chicago Press.

Danziger, Sheldon and Daniel Weinberg. 1994. "The Historical Record: Trends in Family Income, Inequality, and Poverty." In *Confronting Poverty*, edited by S. Danziger, G. Sandefur, and D. Weinberg, pp. 18–50. Cambridge, Mass.: Harvard University Press.

Davis, Kingsley. 1966. "The Role of Class Mobility in Economic Development." In *The Dynamics of Modern Society*, edited by W. J. Goode, pp. 384–91. New York: Atherton.

——. 1984. "Wives and Work." *Population and Development Review* 10: 397–417.

——. 1987. "Low Fertility in Evolutionary Perspective." In *Below-Replacement Fertility in Industrial Societies*, edited by K. Davis, M. Bernstam, and R. Ricardo-Campbell, pp. 48–65. Cambridge: Cambridge University Press.

Denzin, Norman. 1986. "Postmodern Social Theory." *Sociological Theory* 4: 194–204.

——. 1987. "Postmodern Children." *Society* 24: 32–35.

——. 1991. *Images of Postmodern Society*. Newbury Park, Calif.: Sage.

Devereaux, Mary Sue. 1990. "Marital Status." In *Canadian Social Trends*, edited by C. McKie and K. Thompson, pp. 138–41. Toronto, Ontario: Thompson Educational Publishing.

Devine, Joel A. and James D. Wright. 1993. *The Greatest of Evils*. New York: Aldine de Gruyter.

Doyle, Cassie. 1985. "Women and Housing." *Canadian Housing* 2: 22–24.

——. 1991. "The Affordability Divide: Income and Rental Housing Costs in the 1990s." *Canadian Housing* 7: 2–3.

Duskin, Elizabeth, ed. 1990. *Lone-Parent Families*. Paris: Organization for Economic Cooperation and Development.

Economic Council of Canada. 1992. *The New Face of Poverty*. Ottawa, Ontario: Supply and Services Canada.

Elder, Glen. 1977. "Family History and the Life Course." *Journal of Family History* 2: 279–304.

Engeland, John. 1991. "Canadian Renters in Core Housing Need." *Canadian Housing* 7: 6–10.

Evans, Patricia. 1992. "Targeting Single Mothers for Employment." *Social Service Review* 66: 378–98.

Ewald, François. 1983. "Old Age as a Risk." In *Old Age and the Welfare State*, edited by A.-M. Guillemard, pp. 115–25. London: Sage.

Farley, Reynolds. 1994. "Challenges of the 1980s, Challenges for the 1990s." *Footnotes* 22(9): 4–5.

Featherstone, Mike. 1988. "In Pursuit of the Postmodern." *Theory, Culture and Society* 5: 195–215.

——. 1989. "Towards a Sociology of Postmodern Culture." In *Social Structure and Culture*, edited by H. Haferkamp, pp. 147–72. New York: Walter de Gruyter.

Filion, Pierre and Trudi Bunting. 1990. *Affordability of Housing in Canada*. Ottawa, Ontario: Minister of Supply and Services.

Fletcher, Ronald. 1988. *The Shaking of the Foundations*. London: Routledge.

Folbre, Nancy. 1994. *Who Pays for the Kids?* New York: Routledge.

Foster, Ann. 1981. "Wives' Earnings as a Factor in Family Net Worth Accumulation." *Monthly Labor Review* 104: 53–57.

Foster, Hal. 1983. *The Anti-Aesthetic*. Port Townsend: Bay Press.

Friedman, Kathie. 1984. "Households as Income-Pooling Units." In *Households and the World-Economy*, edited by J. Smith, I. Wallerstein, and H.-D. Evers, pp. 37–55. Beverly Hills, Calif.: Sage.

Funiciello, Theresa. 1993. *Tyranny of Kindness*. New York: Atlantic Monthly Press.

Gaffikin, Frank and Mike Morrissey. 1992. *The New Unemployed*. London: Zed Books.

Galbraith, John Kenneth. 1958. *The Affluent Society*. Boston, Mass.: Houghton Mifflin.

Garfinkel, Irwin and Sara McLanahan. 1988. "The Feminization of Poverty." In *Poverty and Social Welfare in the United States*, edited by D. Tomaskovic-Devey, pp. 27–52. Boulder, Colo.: Westview Press.

Gauthier, Pierre. 1991. "Canada's Seniors." *Canadian Social Trends* 22: 16–20.

Ghalam, Nancy Zukewich. 1993. "Women in the Workplace." *Canadian Social Trends* 28: 2–6.

Glendinning, Caroline and Jane Millar, eds. 1987. *Women and Poverty in Britain*. Brighton: Wheatsheaf.

Glennon, Lynda. 1979. *Women and Dualism*. New York: Longman.

Glossop, Robert. 1991. "Distributive Justice." In *Childhood as a Social Phenomenon — National Report Canada*, edited by A. Pence, pp. 41–47. Vienna: European Centre for Social Welfare Policy and Research.

Goldberg, Gertrude Schaffner and Eleanor Kremen. 1990. *The Feminization of Poverty*. New York: Praeger.

Goode, William J. 1963. *World Revolution and Family Patterns*. New York: Free Press.

Gordon, Linda and Sara McLanahan. 1991. "Single Parenthood in 1900." *Journal of Family History* 16: 97–116.

Graham, Hilary. 1987. "Women's Poverty and Caring." In *Women and Poverty in Britian*, edited by C. Glendinning and J. Millar, pp. 221–40. Brighton: Wheatsheaf.

Greene, Barbara. 1991. *Canada's Children*. Ottawa, Ontario: Standing Committee on Health and Welfare, Social Affairs, Seniors and the Status of Women.

Gunderson, Morley. 1983. *Economics of Poverty and Income Distribution*. Toronto, Ontario: Butterworths.

Habermas, Jürgen. 1981. "Modernity versus Postmodernity." *New German Critique* 22: 3–14.

Hall, Peter. 1993. "Forces Shaping Urban Europe." *Urban Studies* 30: 883–98.

Hanson, Sandra and Theodora Ooms. 1991. "The Economic Costs and Rewards of Two-Earner, Two-Parent Families." *Journal of Marriage and the Family* 53: 622–34.

Hareven, Tamara. 1982. *Family Time and Industrial Time*. Cambridge: Cambridge University Press.

Harp, John. 1971. "Canada's Rural Poor." In *Poverty in Canada*, edited by J. Harp and J. Hofley, pp. 174–86. Scarborough, Ontario: Prentice-Hall.

Harrington, Michael. 1964. *The Other America*. New York: Macmillan.

——. 1984. *The New American Poverty*. New York: Holt, Rinehart and Winston.

Harvey, David. 1989. *The Condition of Postmodernity*. Oxford: Blackwell.

Hassan, Ihab. 1987. *The Postmodern Turn*. Columbus: Ohio State University Press.

Haveman, Robert. 1987. *Poverty Policy and Poverty Research*. Madison: University of Wisconsin Press.

Hedström, Peter and Stein Ringen. 1987. "Age and Income in Contemporary Society." *Journal of Social Policy* 16: 227–39.

Heller, Agnes. 1990. "Existentialism, Alienation, Postmodernism: Cultural Movements as Vehicles of Change in the Patterns of Everyday Life." In *Postmodern Conditions*, edited by A. Milner, P. Thomson, and C. Worth, pp. 1–13. New York: Berg.

Heller, Peter, Richard Hemming, and Peter Kohnert. 1986. *Aging and Social Expenditure in the Major Industrial Countries, 1980–2025*. Washington, D.C.: International Monetary Fund.

Hofley, John. 1990. "The Long Revolution in Canadian Families." In *The Political Economy of Manitoba*, edited by J. Silver and J. Hull, pp. 171–87. Regina, Saskatchewan: Canadian Plains Research Center.

Höhn, Charlotte and Kurt Lüscher. 1988. "The Changing Family in the Federal Republic of Germany." *Journal of Family Issues* 9: 317–35.

Hudson, Joe and Burt Galaway, eds. 1993. *Single Parent Families*. Toronto, Ontario: Thompson Educational Publishing.

Hughes, James. 1991. "Clashing Demographics." *Housing Policy Debate* 2: 1217–50.

Human Resources Development Canada. 1994. *Improving Social Security in Canada*. Ottawa, Ontario: Human Resources Development Canada.

Hunsley, Terrance, ed. 1992. *Social Policy in the Global Economy*. Kingston, Ontario: Queen's University School of Policy Studies.

Hunter, Robert. 1904. *Poverty*. New York: Grosset and Dunlap.

Inkeles, Alex. 1983. *Exploring Individual Modernity*. New York: Columbia University Press.

Inkeles, Alex and David H. Smith. 1974. *Becoming Modern*. Cambridge, Mass.: Harvard University Press.

Jacobs, Jerry. 1993. "Careers in the US Service Economy." In *Changing Classes*, edited by G. Esping-Andersen, pp. 195–224. Newbury Park, Calif.: Sage.

Jencks, Christopher. 1991. "Is the American Underclass Growing?" In *The Urban Underclass*, edited by C. Jencks and P. Peterson, pp. 28–100. Washington, D.C.: The Brookings Institution.

Jencks, Christopher and Paul Peterson, eds. 1991. *The Urban Underclass*. Washington, D.C.: The Brookings Institution.

Johnson, Clifford, Andrew Sum, and James Weill. 1988. *Vanishing Dreams*. Washington, D.C.: Children's Defense Fund.

Johnson, Paul. 1992. *Income: Pensions, Earnings and Savings in The Third Age*. Dunfermline: The Carnegie United Kingdom Trust.

Jones, Charles, Lorna Marsden, and Lorne Tepperman. 1990. *Lives of Their Own*. Toronto, Ontario: Oxford University Press.

Kasarda, John. 1993. "Urban Industrial Transition and the Underclass." In *The Ghetto Underclass*, edited by W. J. Wilson, pp. 43–64. Newbury Park, Calif.: Sage.

Katz, Michael, ed. 1993. *The "Underclass" Debate*. Princeton, N.J.: Princeton University Press.

Kelso, William. 1994. *Poverty and the Underclass*. New York: New York University Press.

Kingson, Eric and John Williamson. 1991. "Generational Equity or Privatization of Social Security?" *Society* 28: 38–41.

Klodawsky, Fran and Aron Spector. 1988. "New Families, New Housing Needs, New Urban Environments." In *Life Spaces: Gender, Household, Employment*, edited by C. Andrew and B. Moore Milroy, pp. 141–58. Vancouver: University of British Columbia Press.

Kohli, Martin. 1986. "The World We Forgot: A Historical Review of the Life Course." In *Later Life*, edited by V. Marshall, pp. 271–303. Beverly Hills, Calif.: Sage.

Kohli, Martin, Martin Rein, Anne-Marie Guillemard, and Herman van Gunsteren. 1991. *Time For Retirement*. Cambridge: Cambridge University Press.

Lasch, Christopher. 1991. *The True and Only Heaven*. New York: Norton.

Leira, Arnlaug. 1992. *Welfare States and Working Mothers*. Cambridge: Cambridge University Press.

Levitan, Sar, Richard Belous, and Frank Gallo. 1988. *What's Happening to the American Family?* Baltimore, Md.: Johns Hopkins University Press.

Levy, Frank and Richard Michel. 1991. *The Economic Future of American Families*. Washington, D.C.: Urban Institute Press.

Lichter, Daniel and David Eggebeen. 1994. "The Effect of Parental Employment on Child Poverty." *Journal of Marriage and the Family* 56: 633–45.

Liljeström, Rita. 1986. "Gender Systems and the Family." In *Sociology: From Crisis to Science*, vol. 2, edited by U. Himmelstrand, pp. 132–49. London: Sage.

Lindsay, Colin and Shelley Donald. 1988. "Income of Canada's Seniors." *Canadian Social Trends* 10: 20–25.

Lyotard, Jean-François. 1993. *The Postmodern Explained*. Minneapolis: University of Minnesota Press.

Mack, Joanna and Stewart Lansley. 1985. *Poor Britain*. London: Allen and Unwin.

Maclean, Mavis. 1991. *Surviving Divorce*. Basingstoke: Macmillan.

Mann, Michael. 1986. "A Crisis in Stratification Theory?" In *Gender and Stratification*, edited by R. Crompton and M. Mann, pp. 40–56. Cambridge: Polity Press.

Mare, Robert and Christopher Winship. 1991. "Socioeconomic Change and the Decline of Marriage for Blacks and Whites." In *The Urban Underclass*, edited by C. Jencks and P. Peterson, pp. 175–202 . Washington, D.C.: The Brookings Institution.

Marsden, Lorna. 1991. *Children in Poverty*. Ottawa, Ontario: Standing Senate Committee on Social Affairs, Science and Technology.

Marx, Karl. 1977 [1867]. *Capital*. New York: Vintage Books.

Mayer, Susan and Christopher Jencks. 1989. "Poverty and the Distribution of Material Hardship." *Journal of Human Resources* 24: 88–114.

McDaniel, Susan. 1988. "The Changing Canadian Family." In *Changing Patterns: Women in Canada*, edited by S. Burt, L. Code, and L. Dorney, pp. 103–28. Toronto, Ontario: McClelland and Stewart.

McQuaig, Linda. 1993. *The Wealthy Banker's Wife: The Assault on Equality in Canada*. Toronto, Ontario: Penguin.

McQuillan, Kevin. 1988. "Family Change and Family Income in Canada." Part II in *One-Adult and Two-Earner Households and Families*, edited by T. Burch and K. McQuillan. Ottawa, Ontario: Health and Welfare Canada.

——. 1991. "Family Change and Family Income in Ontario." In *Children, Families, and Public Policy in the 90s*, edited by L. Johnson and D. Barnhorst, pp. 153–73. Toronto, Ontario: Thompson.

——. 1992. "Falling Behind: The Income of Lone-Mother Families, 1970–1985." *Canadian Review of Sociology and Anthropology* 29: 511–23.

Mead, Lawrence. 1992. *The New Politics of Poverty*. New York: Basic Books.

——. 1993. "The Logic of Workfare." In *The Ghetto Underclass*, edited by W. J. Wilson, pp. 173–86. Newbury Park, Calif.: Sage.

Millar, Jane. 1988. "The Costs of Marital Breakdown." In *Money Matters*, edited by R. Walker and G. Parker, pp. 99–114. London: Sage.

Miller, S.M. 1971. "Poverty." In *Poverty in Canada*, edited by J. Harp and J. Hofley, pp. 90–100. Scarborough, Ontario: Prentice-Hall.

Miller, S.M. and Pamela Roby. 1968. "Poverty: Changing Social Stratification." In *On Understanding Poverty*, edited by D. Moynihan, pp. 64–84. New York: Basic Books.

Mingione, Enzo. 1993. "The New Urban Poverty and the Underclass." *International Journal of Urban and Regional Research* 17: 324–26.

Mingione, Enzo and Enrica Morlicchio. 1993. "New Forms of Urban Poverty in Italy." *International Journal of Urban and Regional Research* 17: 413–27.

Miron, John. 1989. "Household Formation, Affordability, and Housing Policy." *Population Research and Policy Review* 8: 55–77.

Mitchell, Deborah. 1991. *Income Transfers in Ten Welfare States*. Aldershot: Avebury.

Moon, Marilyn. 1977. *The Measurement of Economic Welfare*. New York: Academic Press.

——. 1993. "Measuring Intergenerational Equity." In *Justice Across Generations*, edited by L. Cohen, pp. 63–76. Washington, D.C.: Public Policy Institute, American Association of Retired Persons.

Moore, Maureen. 1989. "Dual-Earner Families." *Canadian Social Trends* 12: 24–26.

Moore, Wilbert E. 1966. "Aging and the Social System." In *Aging and Social Policy*, edited by J. C. McKinney and F. T. de Vyver, pp. 23–41. New York: Appleton-Century-Crofts.

Morris, Lydia. 1995. *Social Divisions*. London: UCL Press.

Moynihan, Daniel. 1965. *The Negro Family*. Washington, D.C.: U.S. Department of Labor.

Murray, Charles. 1984. *Losing Ground*. New York: Basic.

Myers, Dowell. 1985. "Wives' Earnings and Rising Costs of Homeownership." *Social Science Quarterly* 66: 319–29.

Myles, John. 1980. "The Aged, the State, and the Structure of Inequality." In *Structured Inequality in Canada*, edited by J. Harp and J. Hofley, pp. 317–42. Scarborough, Ontario: Prentice-Hall.

Myrdal, Gunnar. 1944. *An American Dilemma*. New York: Harper and Row.

National Advisory Commission on Rural Poverty. 1968. "The People Left Behind." In *Man Against Poverty*, edited by A. Blaustein and R. Woock, pp. 184–91. New York: Random House.

National Council of Welfare. 1992. *Poverty Profile, 1980–1990*. Ottawa, Ontario: National Council of Welfare.

Nave-Herz, Rosemarie. 1989. "The Significance of the Family and Marriage in the Federal Republic of Germany." In *Family Divisions and Inequalities in Modern Society*, edited by P. Close, pp. 80–91. Basingstoke: Macmillan.

Neugarten, Bernice and Dail Neugarten. 1989. "Policy Issues in an Aging Society." In *The Adult Years*, edited by M. Storandt and G. VandenBos, pp. 147–67. Washington, D.C.: American Psychological Association.

Newman, Katherine. 1993. *Declining Fortunes*. New York: Basic Books.

Nowotny, Helga. 1993. "The Unfinished Agenda of Modernization." *Social Science Information* 32: 5–21.

Oderkirk, Jillian. 1994. "Marriage in Canada." *Canadian Social Trends* 33: 2–7.

Oechsle, Mechtild and Rainer Zoll. 1992. "Young People and Their Ideas on Parenthood." In *European Parents in the 1990s*, edited by U. Björnberg, pp. 45–58. New Brunswick, N.J.: Transaction Books.

O'Higgins, Michael. 1988. "The Allocation of Public Resources to Children and the Elderly in OECD Countries." In *The Vulnerable*, edited by J. Palmer, T. Smeeding, and B. Boyle Torrey, pp. 201–28. Washington, D.C.: Urban Institute Press.

Oppenheimer, Valerie Kincade. 1994. "Women's Rising Employment and the Future of the Family in Industrial Societies." *Population and Development Review* 20: 293–342.

Organization for Economic Cooperation and Development. 1988. *Ageing Populations*. Paris: Organization for Economic Cooperation and Development.

Orshansky, Mollie. 1965. "Counting the Poor." *Social Security Bulletin* 28: 3–26.

Oster, Sharon, Elizabeth Lake, and Conchita Oksman. 1978. *The Definition and Measurement of Poverty*, vol. 1. Boulder, Colo.: Westview Press.

Paglin, Morton. 1980. *Poverty and Transfers In-Kind*. Stanford, Calif.: Hoover Institution Press.

Parliament, Jo-Anne. 1989. "Women Employed Outside the Home." *Canadian Social Trends* 13: 2–6.

Parsons, Talcott. 1951. *The Social System*. New York: Free Press.

———. 1971. "The Normal American Family." In *Readings on the Sociology of the Family*, edited by B. Adams and T. Weirath, pp. 53–66. Chicago: Markham.

Patterson, James. 1981. *America's Struggle Against Poverty 1900–1980*. Cambridge, Mass.: Harvard University Press.

Phipps, Shelley and Thesia Garner. 1994. "Are Equivalence Scales the Same for the United States and Canada?" *Review of Income and Wealth* 40: 1–17.

Picot, Garnett, John Myles, and Ted Wannell. 1990. *Good Jobs/Bad Jobs and the Declining Middle: 1967–1986*. Ottawa, Ontario: Statistics Canada.

Podoluk, Jenny. 1968. *Incomes of Canadians*. Ottawa, Ontario: Dominion Bureau of Statistics.

Power, Chris. 1991. "Social and Economic Background and Class Inequalities in Health Among Young Adults." *Social Science and Medicine* 32: 411–17.

Preston, Samuel. 1984. "Children and the Elderly." *Demography* 21: 435–57.

Qvortrup, Jens. 1991. *Childhood as a Social Phenomenon*. Vienna: European Centre for Social Welfare Policy and Research.

Rashid, Abdul. 1990a. *The Changing Profile of Canadian Families with Low Incomes, 1970–1985*. Ottawa, Ontario: Statistics Canada.

——. 1990b. *Wealth of Married Couples*. Ottawa, Ontario: Statistics Canada.

——. 1990c. "Government Transfer Payments and Family Income." *Perspectives on Labour and Income* 75-OOIE: 50–60.

——. 1994. *Family Income in Canada*. Ottawa, Ontario: Statistics Canada.

Rein, Martin and Lee Rainwater. 1988. "The Public/Private Mix." In *Public/Private Interplay in Social Protection*, edited by M. Rein and L. Rainwater, pp. 3–24. Armonk, N.Y.: M.E. Sharpe.

Repassy, Helga. 1990. "The Policy Aspects of Aging." In *Aiding and Aging*, edited by J. Mogey, pp. 237–42. New York: Greenwood Press.

Rice, James and Michael Prince. 1993. "Lowering the Safety Net and Weakening the Bonds of Nationhood." In *How Ottawa Spends: 1993–94*, edited by S. Phillips, pp. 381–416. Ottawa, Ontario: Carleton University Press.

Richman, Harold and Matthew Stagner. 1986. "Children in an Aging Society." *Daedalus* 115: 171–89.

Robinson, Patricia. 1987. *Women's Work Interruptions*. Ottawa, Ontario: Supply and Services Canada.

Rodgers, Harrell. 1986. *Poor Women, Poor Families*. Armonk, N.Y.: M.E. Sharpe.

Room, Graham, Roger Lawson, and Frank Laczko. 1989. "'New Poverty' in the European Community." *Policy and Politics* 17: 165–76.

Rosenau, Pauline. 1992. *Post-Modernism and the Social Sciences*. Princeton, N.J.: Princeton University Press.

Rosenberg, Sam. 1993. "United States of America." In *Times Are Changing*, edited by G. Bosch, P. Dawkins, and F. Michon, pp. 289–311. Geneva: International Institute for Labour Studies.

Ross, David. 1989. *The Canadian Fact Book on Poverty — 1989*. Ottawa, Ontario: Canadian Council on Social Development.

Ross, David, E. Richard Shillington, and Clarence Lochhead. 1994. *The Canadian Fact Book on Poverty — 1994*. Ottawa, Ontario: Canadian Council on Social Development.

Rowntree, B. Seebohm. 1902. *Poverty*. London: Macmillan.

——. 1937. *The Human Needs of Labour*. London: Longmans.

——. 1941. *Poverty and Progress*. London: Longmans.

Rowntree, B. Seebohm and G.R. Lavers. 1951. *Poverty and the Welfare State*. London: Longmans, Green and Co.

Rubin, Rose and Bobye Riney. 1994. *Working Wives and Dual-Earner Families*. Westport, Conn.: Praeger.

Ruggeri, G., R. Howard, and K. Bluck. 1994. "The Incidence of Low Income among the Elderly." *Canadian Public Policy* 20: 138–51.

Ruggles, Patricia. 1990. *Drawing the Line*. Washington, D.C.: Urban Institute Press.

Saunders, Peter. 1986. *Social Theory and the Urban Question*. New York: Holmes and Meier.

——. 1990. *A Nation of Home Owners*. London: Unwin Hyman.

Schram, Sanford. 1994. "Postindustrial Welfare Policy." *Review of Radical Political Economics* 26: 56–84.

Sen, Amartya. 1981. *Poverty and Famines*. Delhi: Oxford University Press.

Sgritta, Giovanni B. 1989. "Towards a New Paradigm: Family in the Welfare State Crisis." In *Changing Patterns of European Family Life*, edited by K. Boh, M. Bak, C. Clason, M. Pankratova, J. Qvortrup, G. Sgritta and K. Waerness, pp. 71–92. New York: Routledge.

Sgritta, Giovanni and Angelo Saporiti. 1989. "Myth and Reality in the Discovery and Representation of Childhood." In *Family Divisions and Inequalities in Modern Society*, edited by P. Close, pp. 92–111. Basingstoke: Macmillan.

Sharif, Najma and Shelley Phipps. 1994. "The Challenge of Child Poverty." *Canadian Business Economics* 2 (Spring): 17–30.

Shaw, R. Paul. 1986. "Unemployment and Low Family Incomes in Canada." *Canadian Public Policy* 12: 368–86.

Shorter, Edward. 1975. *The Making of the Modern Family*. New York: Basic Books.

Smeeding, Timothy, Michael O'Higgins, and Lee Rainwater, eds. 1990. *Poverty, Inequality and Income Distribution in Comparative Perspective*. London: Harvester Wheatsheaf.

Smeeding, Timothy, Lee Rainwater, Martin Rein, Richard Hauser, and Gaston Schaber. 1990. "Income Poverty in Seven Countries." In *Poverty, Inequality and Income Distribution in Comparative Perspective*, edited by T. Smeeding, M. O'Higgins, and L. Rainwater, pp. 57–76. London: Harvester Wheatsheaf.

Smeeding, Timothy, Barbara Boyle Torrey, and Martin Rein. 1988. "Patterns of Income and Poverty." In *The Vulnerable*, edited by J. Palmer, T. Smeeding, and B. Boyle Torrey, pp. 89–119. Washington, D.C.: Urban Institute Press.

Smith, James. 1988. "Poverty and the Family." In *Divided Opportunities*, edited by G. Sandefur and M. Tienda, pp. 141–72. New York: Plenum Press.

Smolensky, Eugene, Sheldon Danziger, and Peter Gottschalk. 1988. "The Declining Significance of Age in the United States." In *The Vulnerable*, edited by J. Palmer, T. Smeeding, and B. Boyle Torrey, pp. 29–54. Washington, D.C.: Urban Institute Press.

Stacey, Judith. 1990. *Brave New Families*. New York: Basic Books.

Staff of the Chicago Tribune. 1986. *The American Millstone*. Chicago: Contemporary Books.

Statistics Canada. 1984a. *Canada's Young Family Home-Owners*. Ottawa, Ontario: Minister of Supply and Services.

———. 1984b. *Canadian Husband-Wife Families*. Ottawa, Ontario: Minister of Supply and Services.

———. 1992. *Characteristics of Dual-Earner Families 1990*. Ottawa, Ontario: Statistics Canada.

———. 1993. *Income Distributions by Size in Canada 1992*. Ottawa, Ontario: Statistics Canada.

———. 1994. *Family Expenditure in Canada, 1992*. Ottawa, Ontario: Statistics Canada.

Steele, Marion. 1979. *The Demand for Housing in Canada*. Ottawa, Ontario: Minister of Supply and Services.

Stern, Mark. 1993. "Poverty and Family Composition since 1940." In *The "Underclass" Debate*, edited by M. Katz, pp. 220–53. Princeton, N.J.: Princeton University Press.

Stone, Michael. 1993. *Shelter Poverty*. Philadelphia, Pa.: Temple University Press.

Strawn, J. 1992. "The States and the Poor." *Social Policy Report* 6: 1–19.

Ternowetsky, Gordon and Jill Thorn. 1991. *The Decline in Middle Incomes*. Regina, Saskatchewan: University of Regina.

Thomas, Susan. 1994. *Gender and Poverty*. New York: Garland.

Thomson, David. 1989a. "The Welfare State and Generation Conflict." In *Workers Versus Pensioners*, edited by P. Johnson, C. Conrad, and D. Thomson, pp. 33–56. Manchester: Manchester University Press.

———. 1989b. "The Intergenerational Contract — Under Pressure From Population Aging." In *An Aging World*, edited by J. Eekelaar and D. Pearl, pp. 369–87. Oxford: Clarendon Press.

Townsend, Peter. 1957. *The Family Life of Old People*. London: Routledge and Kegan Paul.

———. 1970. "Measures and Explanations of Poverty in High Income and Low Income Countries." In *The Concept of Poverty*, edited by P. Townsend, pp. 1–45. London: Heinemann.

———. 1973. *The Social Minority*. London: Allen Lane.

———. 1974. "Poverty As Relative Deprivation." In *Poverty, Inequality and Class Structure*, edited by D. Wedderburn, pp. 15–41. Cambridge: Cambridge University Press.

———. 1979. *Poverty in the United Kingdom*. Berkeley: University of California Press.

———. 1987. "Deprivation." *Journal of Social Policy* 16: 125–46.

U.S. Bureau of the Census. 1991. *Current Population Reports, Series P–60, No. 176-RD, Measuring the Effect of Benefits and Taxes on Income and Poverty: 1990*. Washington, D.C.: U.S. Government Printing Office.

———. 1993. *Poverty in the United States: 1992*. Washington, D.C.: U.S. Government Printing Office.

U.S. Bureau of Labor Statistics. 1993. *Consumer Expenditure Survey, 1990–91*. Washington, D.C.: U.S. Government Printing Office.

U.S. General Accounting Office. 1990. *The Urban Underclass*. Washington, D.C.: U.S. General Accounting Office.

———. 1992. *Poverty Trends, 1980–88*. Washington, D.C.: U.S. General Accounting Office.

van Kempen, Eva. 1994. "The Dual City and the Poor." *Urban Studies* 31: 995–1015.

van Vliet, Willem. 1983. "Families in Apartment Buildings." *Environment and Behavior* 15: 211–34.

van Vucht Tijssen, Lieteke. 1990. "Women between Modernity and Postmodernity." In *Theories of Modernity and Postmodernity*, edited by B. Turner, pp. 147–63. Newbury Park, Calif.: Sage.

Vastel, Michel. 1994. "Quebec: The Politics of Survival." *Transition* 24: 15, 20.

Veit-Wilson, J.H. 1987. "Consensual Approaches to Poverty Lines and Social Security." *Journal of Social Policy* 16: 183–211.

Vickery, Clair. 1979. "Women's Economic Contribution to the Family." In *The Subtle Revolution*, edited by R. Smith, pp. 159–200. Washington, D.C.: The Urban Institute.

Voydanoff, Patricia. 1990. "Economic Distress and Family Relations." *Journal of Marriage and the Family* 52: 1099–1115.

Wagner, Peter. 1994. *A Sociology of Modernity*. New York: Routledge.

Watson, Sophie. 1986. "Women and Housing or Feminist Housing Analysis?" *Housing Studies* 1: 1–10.

Weinberg, Daniel. 1985. "Filling the 'Poverty Gap'." *Journal of Human Resources* 20: 64–89.

Wilk, Richard, ed. 1989. *The Household Economy*. Boulder, Colo.: Westview Press.

Wilson, William Julius. 1987. *The Truly Disadvantaged*. Chicago: University of Chicago Press.

Wisensale, Steven. 1992. "Toward the 21st Century: Family Change and Public Policy." *Family Relations* 41: 417–22.

Wolfe, Barbara. 1991. "Treating Children Fairly." *Society* 28: 23–28.

Zelizer, Viviana. 1979. *Morals and Markets*. New York: Columbia University Press.

Zill, Nicholas and Carolyn Rogers. 1988. "Recent Trends in the Well-Being of Children in the United States and Their Implications for Public Policy." In

The Changing American Family and Public Policy, edited by A. Cherlin, pp. 31–115. Washington, D.C.: Urban Institute Press.

Zill, Nicholas and Christine Winquist Nord. 1994. *Running In Place*. Washington, D.C.: Child Trends, Inc.

Zopf, Paul. 1989. *American Women in Poverty*. New York: Greenwood Press.

Index

ABOUT THE AUTHOR

David Cheal is a Professor of Sociology, University of Winnipeg. Among his earlier publications are *The Gift Economy* (1988) and *Family and the State of Theory* (1991).

ISBN 0-313-29444-5

9 0 0 0 0 >

EAN

9 780313 294440

HARDCOVER BAR CODE